OCS EIS/EA
MMS 2008-003

Proposed Gulf of Mexico OCS Oil and Gas Lease Sale 207

Western Planning Area

Environmental Assessment

Author

Minerals Management Service
Gulf of Mexico OCS Region

U.S. Department of the Interior
Minerals Management Service
Gulf of Mexico OCS Region

New Orleans
March 2008

FINDING OF NO NEW SIGNIFICANT IMPACT

The U.S. Department of the Interior, Minerals Management Service (MMS) has prepared an environmental assessment (EA) for proposed Lease Sale 207 in the Western Planning Area (WPA) of the Gulf of Mexico (GOM) Outer Continental Shelf (OCS) to determine whether MMS can make a Finding of No New Significant Impact (FONNSI) or should prepare a supplemental environmental impact statement (EIS).

In April 2007, MMS filed with the U.S. Environmental Protection Agency a Final EIS covering WPA Lease Sales 204, 207, 210, 215, and 218 and Central Planning Area (CPA) Lease Sales 205, 206, 208, 213, 216, and 222 in the GOM (Multisale EIS) (USDOI, MMS, 2007a). Because the Multisale EIS examined the environmental impacts of a sale similar in size, nature, and potential level of development as proposed Lease Sale 207, the EA tiers off the Multisale EIS and incorporates much of the material by reference. It also reexamines the potential environmental effects of proposed Lease Sale 207 and the alternatives based on any new information regarding potential impacts or issues that were not available at the time the Multisale EIS was prepared.

The purpose of the EA is to analyze whether new information indicates that there are likely to be significant new impacts that were not addressed in the Multisale EIS. As part of the scoping process for the EA, MMS researched and reviewed new information to determine if any resources should be reevaluated or if the new information would alter conclusions of the Multisale EIS. No new information was found that would necessitate a reanalysis of the impacts of proposed Lease Sale 207 upon environmental or socioeconomic resources. The analyses and potential impacts detailed in the Multisale EIS apply for proposed Lease Sale 207. New information was found that further supports or elaborates on analyses or information presented in the Multisale EIS, but it does not change the conclusions of any of the analyses in the Multisale EIS.

Based on the analyses in the EA, no new significant impacts were identified for proposed Lease Sale 207 that were not already assessed in the Multisale EIS, nor is it necessary to change the conclusions of the kinds, levels, or locations of impacts described in that document. Therefore, MMS has determined that a supplemental EIS is not required and is issuing this FONNSI.

Supporting Document

Gulf of Mexico OCS Oil and Gas Lease Sales: 2007-2012: Western Planning Area Sales 204, 207, 210, 215, and 218; Central Planning Area Sales 205, 206, 208, 213, 216, and 222—Final Environmental Impact Statement; Volumes I and II (available upon request and at http://www.gomr.mms.gov/homepg/regulate/environ/ncpa/nepaprocess.html)

Walter D Cruickshank
Acting   Director

3/07/08
Date

TABLE OF CONTENTS

FIGURES

TABLES

1. OBJECTIVES OF THE ENVIRONMENTAL ASSESSMENT

This environmental assessment (EA) addresses one proposed Federal action: oil and gas Lease Sale 207 in the proposed lease sale area of the Western Planning Area (WPA) of the Gulf of Mexico (GOM) Outer Continental Shelf (OCS) as scheduled in the *Outer Continental Shelf Oil and Gas Leasing Program 2007-2012* (5-Year Program) (USDOI, MMS, 2007b). This EA incorporates by reference all of the relevant material in the multisale environmental impact statement (EIS) from which it tiers (i.e., *Gulf of Mexico OCS Oil and Gas Lease Sales: 2007-2012; Western Planning Area Sales 204, 207, 210, 215, and 218; Central Planning Area Sales 205, 206, 208, 213, 216, and 222—Final Environmental Impact Statement; Volumes I and II* (Multisale EIS) (USDOI, MMS, 2007a)). The EA has been prepared to aid in the determination of whether or not new available information indicates that the proposed lease sale would result in new significant impacts not addressed in the Multisale EIS.

In preparation for this EA, the U.S. Department of the Interior (USDOI), Minerals Management Service (MMS) reexamined the potential environmental effects of proposed Lease Sale 207 and the alternatives based on any new information regarding potential impacts and issues not available at the time MMS published the Multisale EIS in April 2007. New information was reviewed to determine if any resources should be reevaluated or if the new information would alter conclusions of the Multisale EIS. No new information was found that would necessitate a reanalysis of the impacts of proposed Lease Sale 207 upon any of the environmental or socioeconomic resources. The analyses and potential impacts detailed in the Multisale EIS apply for proposed Lease Sale 207. New information was found that further supports or elaborates on the analyses or information presented in the Multisale EIS, but it does not change the conclusions of any of the analyses in the Multisale EIS.

Federal regulations allow for an agency to analyze related or similar proposals in one EIS (40 CFR 1502.4). The MMS prepared a single EIS for the five WPA lease sales because Lease Sales 204, 207, 210, 215, and 218 and their projected activities are very similar, especially with respect to impact-producing factors. The Multisale EIS approach focuses the National Environmental Policy Act (NEPA) EIS process on the differences between the proposed lease sales and new information and issues. Although the Multisale EIS addressed five proposed WPA lease sale actions, the Secretary of the Interior (Secretary) makes a separate decision for each lease sale.

The Multisale EIS can be obtained from the Minerals Management Service, Gulf of Mexico OCS Region, Attention: Public Information Office (MS 5034), 1201 Elmwood Park Boulevard, Room 114, New Orleans, Louisiana 70123-2394 (1-800-200-GULF) or viewed on the MMS website at http://www.gomr.mms.gov. A list of libraries and other repositories that have copies of the Multisale EIS and their locations is also available on the MMS Internet website at http://www.gomr.mms.gov/homepg/regulate/environ/libraries.html.

2. PURPOSE OF AND NEED FOR THE PROPOSED ACTION

Purpose of the Proposed Action

The purpose of this proposed action (WPA Lease Sale 207) is to offer for lease all unleased blocks in the proposed lease sale area (**Figure 1**) that may contain economically recoverable oil and natural gas resources. The proposed lease sale would provide qualified bidders the opportunity to bid upon and lease acreage in the proposed lease sale area in order to explore, develop, and produce oil and natural gas.

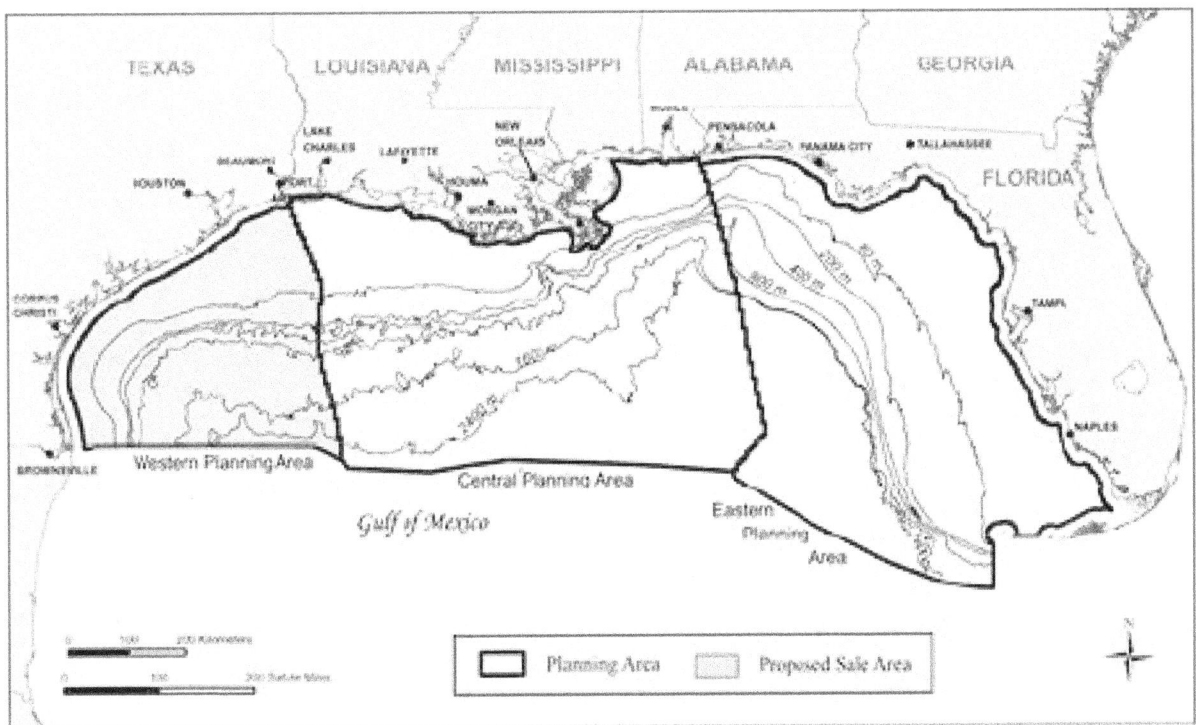

Figure 1. Gulf of Mexico Outer Continental Shelf Planning Areas, Proposed Lease Sale Area, and Locations of Major Cities.

Need for the Proposed Action

The GOM constitutes one of the world's major oil- and gas-producing areas and has proved to be a steady and reliable source of crude oil and natural gas for more than 50 years. Oil from the GOM would help reduce the quantity of oil imported from distant and volatile oil-producing regions of the world and would help reduce the environmental risks associated with overseeing the transport of oil in tankers. Natural gas is not transported easily, making domestic production especially desirable. Gas is generally considered to be an environmentally preferable alternative to oil for generating electricity, a common and growing use for natural gas.

3. ALTERNATIVES INCLUDING THE PROPOSED ACTION

3.1. ALTERNATIVE A—PROPOSED ACTION

Alternative A (Preferred Alternative)—The Proposed Action: This alternative would offer for lease all unleased blocks within the WPA for oil and gas operations (**Figure 2**), with the following exceptions: (1) whole and partial blocks that are within the boundary of the Flower Garden Banks National Marine

Sanctuary; and (2) whole and partial blocks that lie within the 1.4-nautical mile (nmi) buffer zone north of the continental shelf boundary between the U.S. and Mexico for Sales 204, 207, 210, and 215 only.

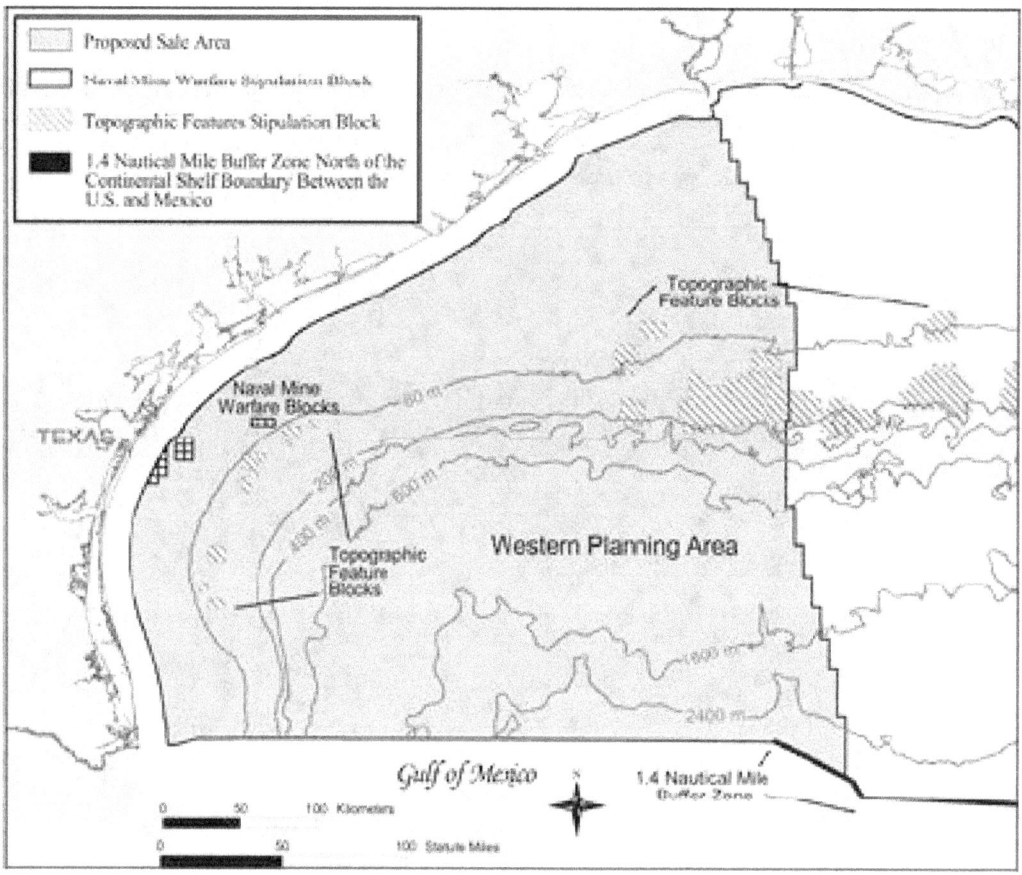

Figure 2.   Location of Proposed Stipulations and Deferrals.

The WPA sale area encompasses about 28.6 million ac located 3 leagues (9 mi) offshore Texas and extends to the limits of the U.S. Outer Continental Shelf where water depths are up to 10,978 ft (3,346 m) deep.   The estimated amount of resources projected to be developed as a result of one proposed WPA lease sale is 0.242-0.423 billion barrels of oil (BBO) and 1.644-2.647 trillion cubic feet (Tcf) of gas (USDOI, MMS, 2007a; Table 4-1).

The analyses of impacts summarized below and described in detail in Chapters 4.2.1.1and 4.4 of the Multisale EIS are based on the development scenario, which is a set of assumptions and estimates on the amounts, locations, and timing for OCS exploration, development, and production operations and facilities, both offshore and onshore. A detailed discussion of the development scenario and major related offshore, coastal, and accidental impact-producing factors is included in Chapters 4.1.1, 4.1.2, and 4.3 of the Multisale EIS.

3.2.   ALTERNATIVES TO THE PROPOSED ACTION

Alternative B—The Proposed Action Excluding the Unleased Blocks Near Biologically Sensitive Topographic Features: This alternative would offer for lease all unleased blocks in the WPA, as described for the proposed action for Alternative A, and in addition exclude all other blocks in the WPA subject to the Topographic Features stipulation. A detailed analysis of Alternative B is presented in Chapter 4.2.1.2 of the Multisale EIS.

Alternative C—Use of a Nomination and Tract Selection Leasing System: A detailed analysis of Alternative C is presented in Chapter 4.2.1.4 of the Multisale EIS.   This alternative addressed a very specific scenario that would limit the number of blocks offered for lease for proposed Lease Sale 207, potentially reducing the total number of blocks leased.

Since the publication of the Multisale EIS, MMS has awarded a contract to an outside contractor to study alternative approaches to leasing that may serve better the many goals of the OCSLA. This MMS-funded study, in conjunction with MMS review and assessment of its policy implications, is expected to take 2-3 years. The MMS will provide the contractor with all of the comments received on alternatives to areawide leasing. If it is determined that one or more alternative approaches to leasing is preferable, the 5-Year Program could be adjusted accordingly or it can be incorporated into the subsequent 5-Year Program.

Until the study and its assessment are complete, MMS must be cautious regarding the effects that any policy changes might have on the achievement of other statutory and implicit goals of the Federal OCS Program. Among these goals are expeditious and orderly development of the natural resources of the OCS and maintaining a diverse and competitive industry. Areawide leasing allows smaller independent companies to timely acquire and rapidly produce low-resource, low-risk fields, while inducing larger companies to develop state-of-the-art technology to explore and develop deepwater prospects. It also encourages strong and innovative seismic exploration and geophysical contracting and processing industries. In addition, a sudden change in policy that restricts access to oil and gas resources or that alters the timetables the offshore industry has come to expect and depend upon may lead to undesirable socioeconomic disruptions in local coastal economies.

Alternative D—No Action: This alternative is the cancellation of WPA Lease Sale 207. The opportunity for development of the estimated 0.242-0.432 BBO and 1.644-2.647 Tcf of gas that could have resulted from a proposed WPA lease sale would be precluded or postponed. Any potential environmental impacts resulting from a proposed lease sale would not occur or would be postponed. Other sources of energy would substitute for the lost production. Principal substitutes would be additional imports, conservation, additional domestic production, and switching to other fuels. These alternatives, except conservation, have significant negative environmental impacts of their own, which are analyzed in the Final EIS for the 5-Year Program (USDOI, MMS, 2007c).

3.3.   MITIGATION MEASURES

Proposed Lease Sale 207 and all subsequent activities resulting from it are subject to the existing regulations and proposed lease stipulations designed to reduce environmental risks. Lease stipulations are legally binding restrictions and operating requirements that, if adopted, become part of lease contracts. Chapter 4.3.1.3 of the Multisale EIS analyzed four environmental or military stipulations proposed to be applied to leases resulting from WPA Lease Sale 207: Topographic Features; the Military Areas; the Protected Species; and the Operations in the Naval Mine Warfare Area. The Law of the Sea Convention Royalty Payment stipulation is also applicable to Lease Sale 207, although it is not an environmental or military stipulation.

Chapter 2.4.1.3 of the Multisale EIS discusses the effectiveness of these stipulations. Additional stipulations or mitigation requirements to be included in Lease Sale 207 will be described in the Final Notice of Sale for Lease Sale 207.

3.3.1.   Summary of Stipulations Discussed in the Multisale EIS

Four environmental and military mitigations, referred to as lease stipulations, were included for analysis in the Multisale EIS. These stipulations were developed as the result of scoping efforts over a number of years for the continuing OCS Program in the GOM and are expected to be part of the proposed action if Sale 207 goes forward. These stipulations and their effectiveness are described in more detail in Chapter 2 of the Multisale EIS. Any stipulations or mitigation requirements to be included in Lease Sale 207 will be described in detail in the Final Notice of Sale for Lease Sale 207. Stipulations or mitigation requirements, in addition to those analyzed in the Multisale EIS, can also be developed and applied, and they will also be described in the Final Notice of Sale. The following environmental and military stipulations are applicable to Lease Sale 207:

- The **Topographic Features Stipulation** explains what blocks are excluded from Alternative A and why (Chapter 2.3.1.3.1 of the Multisale EIS).

- The **Operations in the Naval Mine Warfare Area** includes blocks considered crucial to the Naval Mine and Anti-Submarine Warfare Command operations that were at one time deferred from leasing. The MMS has been informed by the Navy that these blocks are still used for testing equipment and for training mine warfare personnel; however, the Navy does not object to these blocks being offered for lease under the condition of no surface occupancy. Parts of blocks in the Mustang Island Area include Blocks 768, 769, 775, 777, 778, 790, 791, 793, 798, 799, 815, 816, 821, and 822; and Mustang Island Area East Addition Blocks 732, 733, and 734. The no surface occupancy condition could change; however, a consultation with the Commander, Mine Warfare Command, would be required prior to the submission of an Exploration Plan or Development Operations Coordination Document and a revision to the applicable stipulation would follow. Therefore, MMS proposes to offer Mustang Island Blocks 793, 799, and 816 for lease in WPA Lease Sale 207. See Chapter 2.3.1.3.3 of the Multisale EIS for more information on this stipulation.

- The **Military Areas Stipulation** has been applied to all blocks leased in military areas since 1977 and reduces potential impacts, particularly in regards to safety, but does not reduce or eliminate the actual physical presence of oil and gas operations in areas where military operations are conducted. The lessee agrees to control its own electromagnetic emissions and those of its agents, employees, invitees, and independent contractors to prevent damage to, or unacceptable interference with, Department of Defense flight, testing, or operational activities, conducted within individual designated warning areas. The stipulation contains a "hold harmless" clause (holding the U.S. Government harmless in case of an accident involving military operations) and requires lessees to enter into an agreement with the commander of the individual command headquarters to coordinate their activities with appropriate contacts. See Chapter 2.3.1.3.2 of the Multisale EIS for more information on this stipulation.

- The **Protected Species Stipulation** has been applied to all blocks leased in the GOM since December 2001. This stipulation was developed in consultation with the U.S. Department of Commerce (USDOC), National Oceanic and Atmospheric Administration (NOAA), National Marine Fisheries Service (NMFS), and U.S. Fish and Wildlife Service (FWS) in accordance with Section 7 of the Endangered Species Act of 1973 (ESA) and is designed to minimize or avoid potential adverse impacts on federally protected species. See Chapter 2.3.1.3.4 of the Multisale EIS for more information on this stipulation.

- The **Law of the Sea Convention Royalty Payment** includes whole blocks and portions of blocks that lie within the former Western Gap portion of the 1.4 nautical mile buffer zone north of the continental shelf boundary between the United States and Mexico and includes the following blocks: Keathley Canyon (Map Number NG15-05), portions of Blocks 978 through 980; Sigsbee Escarpment (Map Number NG15-08), whole Blocks 11, 57, 103, 148, 149, 194 and portions of Blocks 12 through 14, 58 through 60, 104 through 106, and 150.

  Although not a military or environmental stipulation, the Law of the Sea Convention Royalty Payment stipulation was included in the Final Notice of Sale for Western Lease Sales 204 and 206, and for CPA Lease Sale 205. For completeness, it is mentioned here as applicable to Lease Sale 207.

3.3.2. Existing Mitigations

Chapter 2.2.2.2 of the Multisale EIS discusses mitigations that would be applied by MMS. Mitigations have been identified, evaluated, or developed through previous MMS lease sale NEPA review and analysis. Many of these mitigations have been adopted and incorporated into regulations and/or guidelines governing OCS exploration, development, and production activities. The MMS rigorously reviews all plans for OCS activities (e.g., exploration and development plans, pipeline applications, and structure-removal applications) to ensure compliance with established laws and regulations. Existing mitigations must be incorporated and documented in plans submitted to MMS. The MMS enforces operational compliance with these mitigations through the MMS on-site inspection program.

Mitigations that are a standard part of the MMS program ensure that the operations are always conducted in an environmentally sound manner. For example, mitigations ensure that site-clearance procedures eliminate potential snags to commercial fishing nets and require surveys to detect and avoid archaeological sites and biologically-sensitive areas such as topographic features and chemosynthetic communities.

Mitigations identified by MMS are incorporated into OCS operations through cooperative agreements or efforts with industry and various State and Federal agencies. These mitigations include NMFS's Observer Program to protect marine mammals and sea turtles during explosive removals, labeling operational supplies to track possible sources of accidental debris loss, development of methods of pipeline landfall to eliminate impacts on barrier beaches, and semiannual beach cleanup events.

Site-specific mitigations are also applied by MMS during plan reviews. The MMS determined that many of these site-specific mitigations were consistently applied and used these to develop a list of "standard" mitigations. There are currently over 120 standard mitigations. The wording of a standard mitigation is developed by MMS in advance and may be applied whenever conditions warrant. Standard mitigation text is revised as often as necessary (e.g., to reflect changes in regulatory citations, agency/personnel contact numbers, and internal policy). Site-specific mitigation categories include air quality, archaeological resources, artificial reef material, chemosynthetic communities, Flower Garden Banks, topographic features, military warning areas, Naval mine warfare areas, hydrogen sulfide, drilling hazards, remotely operated vehicle surveys, geophysical survey reviews, and general safety concerns. Site-specific mitigation types include advisories, conditions of approval, hazard survey reviews, inspection requirements, notifications, post-approval submittals, reminders, and safety precautions. In addition to standard mitigations, MMS may also apply nonrecurring mitigations that are developed on a case-by-case basis.

Compensatory mitigation does exist for OCS-related impacts as discussed in Chapter 3.3.5.2 of the Multisale EIS. In addition to over $1 billion Louisiana has received from Federal offshore 8(g) revenues from Fiscal Years (FY) 1986-2005, the State received millions of dollars from the Land and Water Conservation Fund ($469,166 in FY 2006) and the National Historic Preservation Fund ($629,567 in FY 2006).

Section 384 of the Energy Policy Act of 2005 established the Coastal Impact Assistance Program (CIAP), which authorizes funds to be distributed to OCS oil- and gas-producing states to mitigate the impacts of OCS oil and gas activities. Under CIAP, the Secretary of the Interior is authorized to distribute $250 million for each of the fiscal years 2007 through 2010 to producing States and coastal political subdivisions. Although CIAP will be a funding source administered by MMS, it is the responsibility of local and State agencies to submit projects for funding consideration. This money will be shared among Alabama, Alaska, California, Louisiana, Mississippi, and Texas and shall be used for one or more of the following purposes:

- projects and activities for the conservation, protection, or restoration of coastal areas, including wetlands;

- mitigation of damage to fish, wildlife, or natural resources;

- planning assistance and the administrative costs of complying with this section;

- implementation of a federally-approved marine, coastal, or comprehensive conservation management plan; and

- mitigation of the impact of OCS activities through funding of onshore infrastructure projects and public service needs.

Beginning in 2017, the Gulf of Mexico Energy Security Act of 2006 (GOMESA) provides for the sharing of qualified OCS revenues from all Gulf leases issued after December 20, 2006. In accordance with GOMESA, Texas, Louisiana, Mississippi, and Alabama will receive additional OCS revenues from leases issued as a result of WPA Lease Sale 207 beginning in 2017. The Act states these funds are also to be used for the purposes listed above.

The MMS requested an opinion from the Department of the Interior, Office of the Solicitor (SOL), regarding MMS's authority to collect fees from OCS leaseholders and operators for use in mitigating onshore impacts of OCS activities. The SOL determined that MMS does not have the regulatory authority to assess fees for compensatory mitigation nor has it had this authority in the past. Unless Congress specifically earmarks funds for such purposes (e.g., GOMESA (revenue sharing), the Energy Policy Act of 2005 (CIAP funding), the Land and Water Conservation Fund, and the National Historic Preservation Fund), revenue collected by MMS must go to the general fund.

The MMS participates in the Louisiana Sand Management Working Group (LA-SMWG), which is composed of representatives from Federal, State, and local governments, academia, and industry, and serves to assist all parties in planning and decisionmaking for the use of Federal sand for beach nourishment, coastal restoration, and wetlands protection projects along the Louisiana coast. Since the first meeting in 2003, the LA-SMWG has evolved to act as a general forum to discuss issues related to coastal restoration and OCS sand resources. Although LA-SMWG does not distribute compensatory mitigation for coastal impacts, it does serve as a means for parties that are planning projects under CIAP (e.g., to better understand the requirements for accessing OCS sand). The last meeting of the group was on November 29, 2007, at the Lindy Boggs Center at the University of New Orleans.

3.3.3. Notices to Lessees and Operators

The MMS issues Notices to Lessees and Operators (NTL's) to provide clarification, description, or interpretation of a regulation; to provide guidelines on the implementation of a special lease stipulation or regional requirement; or to convey administrative information. A detailed listing of current GOM OCS Region NTL's is available through the MMS, GOM OCS Region's Internet website at http://www.gomr.mms.gov/homepg/regulate/regs/ntls/ntl_lst.html or through the Region's Public Information Office at (504) 736-2519 or 1-800-200-GULF. The MMS issued several NTL's related to the 2007 hurricane season, which are discussed in **Chapter 4.1.3.** Several NTL's provide guidance on monitoring requirements and are described in the following section.

3.3.4. Monitoring

The MMS requires post-activity submittals for several activities, including seismic surveys and installation and decommissioning operations. Post-activity submittals allow MMS to monitor compliance with mitigations and to determine the effectiveness of those mitigations. The MMS is continually revising applicable mitigations to allow the GOM Region to more easily and routinely track mitigation compliance and effectiveness. A primary focus of this effort is requiring post-approval submittal of information within a specified timeframe after a triggering event that is currently tracked by MMS (e.g., end of operations reports for plans, construction reports for pipelines, and removal reports for structure removals).

In addition to compliance monitoring, MMS's Environmental Studies and Research Monitoring involves a repeated sampling of the environment over time to establish baseline conditions, determine natural variability, and assess changes and trends due to human activities. The MMS conducts this type of monitoring through its Environmental Studies Program to determine the extent to which activities caused by or permitted by MMS, such as development of offshore oil and gas, sand and gravel, and methane hydrate resources, affect the human, marine, and coastal environments. As a part of the Environmental Studies Program, the GOM Region has funded more than 350 completed or ongoing environmental studies.

The following describes some of these monitoring activities.

Protected Species NTL's

The Protected Species Stipulation is embodied in NTL's 2007-G02, 2007-G03, and 2007-G04, which instruct lessees and operators on how to implement these mitigations.

Implementation of Seismic Survey Mitigation Measures and Protected Species Observer Program (NTL 2007-G02)

NTL 2007-G02, "Implementation of Seismic Survey Mitigation Measures and Protected Species Observer Program," details information on ramp-up procedures, observation methods, and reporting requirements to be followed by the seismic industry during certain geological and geophysical survey operations. The conditions prescribed under the NTL aid in reducing the chance of harassment to nearby marine mammals and sea turtles. The report data received from the companies is being used by MMS to monitor the effectiveness of current mitigations.

Marine Trash and Debris Awareness and Elimination (NTL 2007-G03)

NTL 2007-G03, "Marine Trash and Debris Awareness and Elimination," provides guidance to prevent intentional and/or accidental introduction of debris into the marine environment. Operators are prohibited from deliberately discharging containers and other similar materials (i.e., trash and debris) into the marine environment (30 CFR 250.300(a) and (b)(6)) and are required to make durable identification markings on equipment, tools, containers (especially drums), and other material (30 CFR 250.300(c)). An annual report that describes the marine trash and debris awareness training process and certifies that the training process has been followed for the previous calendar year is to be provided to MMS by January 31 of each year.

Vessel Strike Avoidance and Injured/Dead Protected Species Reporting (NTL 2007-G04)

NTL 2007-G04, "Vessel Strike Avoidance and Injured/Dead Protected Species Reporting," explains how operators must implement measures to minimize the risk of vessel strikes to protected species and report observations of injured or dead protected species. Vessel operators and crews must maintain a vigilant watch for marine protected species and slow down or stop their vessel to avoid striking protected species. Crews must report sightings of any injured or dead protected species (marine mammals and sea turtles) immediately, regardless of whether the injury or death is caused by their vessel, to the Marine Mammal and Sea Turtle Stranding Hotline or the Marine Mammal Stranding Network. In addition, if it was their own vessel that collided with a protected species, MMS must be notified within 24 hours of the strike.

The importance of accurate and complete reporting of the results of the mitigations cannot be overstated. Only through diligent and careful reporting can MMS, and subsequently NMFS, determine the need for and effectiveness of mitigations. Information on observer effort and seismic operations are as important as animal sighting and behavior data.

Biologically Sensitive Areas of the Gulf of Mexico (NTL 2004-G05)

The Topographic Features Stipulation is embodied in the comprehensive NTL 2004-G05, "Biologically Sensitive Areas of the Gulf of Mexico." In addition to existing stipulated areas for biological features, this NTL establishes a new category of protected area termed "Potentially Sensitive Biological Features." These are hard-bottom features not protected by a biological lease stipulation that are of moderate to high relief (about 8 ft (2.4 m) or higher), provide surface area for the growth of sessile invertebrates, and have the potential to attract large numbers of fish. These features would be located outside any "No Activity Zone" of any of the named topographic features (banks) stipulated blocks. Following the completion of any activity that proposed disturbance of the seafloor within a specified distance of topographic features or potentially sensitive biological features, operators must submit a map showing the location of the seafloor disturbance relative to these features.

Site Clearance (NTL 98-26)

NTL 98-26, "Minimum Interim Requirements for Site Clearance (and Verification) of Abandoned Oil and Gas Structures in the GOM," provides the requirements and guidelines for removing bottom debris and gear after structure decommissioning and removal operations. These mitigations ensure that site-clearance procedures eliminate potential snags to commercial fishing nets and require surveys to detect and avoid archaeological sites and biologically-sensitive areas such as topographic features and chemosynthetic communities.

Once all bottom-founded components are severed and the structures/wells are removed, operators must verify that the seafloor is clear of obstructions and the site has been returned to prelease conditions. Platforms are cleared within a 1,320-foot-radius circle (400 m) centered on the platform geometric center. Single well caisson and well protectors are cleared within an area of a 600-foot-radius circle (183 m) centered on the well.

Site-clearance verification must take place within 60 days after structure-removal operations have been conducted. Procedures include sonar surveys and/or trawling the cleared site by a licensed "shrimp" trawler to ensure that no "hangs" exist.

Remotely Operated Vehicle Surveys (NTL 2003-G03)

On January 23, 2003, MMS issued NTL 2003-G03, "Remotely Operated Vehicle (ROV) Surveys in Deepwater." The NTL provides guidance for ROV surveys and reports in water depths greater than 400 m (1,312 ft). Eighteen grid areas were developed to ensure a broad and systematic analysis of deep water and to depict areas of biological similarity, primarily on the basis of benthic communities. The grid areas cover the WPA sale area and CPA sale area, with the exception of the easternmost portion.

Operators must submit a ROV survey plan with each exploration plan submitted in each grid area and with the Development Operations Coordination Document for the first surface structure proposed in each grid area. The ROV surveys will serve several purposes. In addition to monitoring the effects of the particular plans for which they are required, the surveys will improve our overall knowledge of benthic habitats in deep water and provide more information on the seafloor in deep water. The surveys will also provide information on the distribution and accumulation of mud and cuttings and thereby possibly help us to develop and refine mitigations.

Seafloor Monitoring

The Seafloor Monitoring Program in the GOM Region began in 1997 as a way to assess industry compliance with mitigations applied to offshore activities, which typically consist of avoidance criteria of seafloor features. The Seafloor Monitoring Program Team is comprised of a pool of scientific divers from MMS that, since its inception, has ranged in number from five to eight members. At present, the team consists of three biologists, two archaeologists, and one geophysicist. In addition to monitoring industry compliance with environmental mitigations, the Seafloor Monitoring Team also supports the MMS Environmental Studies Program by conducting contract inspections and oversight of fieldwork.

Over the last 10 years (1997 through 2006), the Seafloor Monitoring Team has completed 53 field investigations to verify archaeological and biological mitigations, to inspect industry activity on pipeline and well-site construction, and to support the MMS Environmental Studies Program.

Long-term Monitoring at the Flower Garden Banks National Marine Sanctuary

Following the designation of the Flower Garden Banks as a National Marine Sanctuary in 1992, MMS, in a partnership with NMFS and through consultation with academia and industry, implemented a program to monitor changes in coral populations and growth, as well as explore other important factors associated with these reefs. These monitoring studies have demonstrated that the shunting requirements of the Topographic Features Stipulation are effective in preventing the muds and cuttings from impacting the biota of the banks. Through establishment of the Flower Garden Banks National Marine Sanctuary, MMS made substantial progress in implementing many of the recommendations of previous monitoring reports.

During the 1998-2001 period, analysis of monitoring data indicated that the Flower Garden Banks were healthy and productive (Dokken et al., 2003). This monitoring effort was designed to assess the health of the coral reefs, evaluate changes in coral population levels, measure coral and algae cover and growth rates, and investigate other community characteristics. The goal of the program is to address concerns related to both gradual and punctuated degradation of these unique offshore ecosystems. Such data are useful in assessing the impacts of industrial activities, as well as their value to resource management. No significant impact from oil/gas production activity has been documented after Sanctuary designation.

Long-term monitoring has continued on a yearly basis at both banks through an equal partnership with MMS and NMFS. This monitoring not only expands MMS's knowledge and understanding of the Flower Garden Banks ecosystem, but it also improves the foundation from which management decisions are made.

In addition, another MMS study, *Post-Hurricane Assessment of Sensitive Habitats of the Flower Garden Banks Vicinity* (Precht et al., in preparation (a)), is investigating hurricane effects at the East Flower Garden, Sonnier, McGrail, Geyer, and Bright Banks.

Inspection Program

The Outer Continental Shelf Lands Act (OCSLA) authorizes and requires MMS to provide for both an annual scheduled inspection and a periodic unscheduled (unannounced) inspection of all oil and gas operations on the OCS. The GOM Region has an extensive, detailed inspection program to ensure safe and environmentally sound offshore oil and gas operations. This program places MMS inspectors offshore on drilling rigs and production platforms on a daily basis on weekdays, weather permitting, as well as on weekends on an as-needed basis, to assure compliance with all regulatory constraints that allowed commencement of the operation.

4. RESOURCES AND IMPACT ANALYSIS

4.1. UPDATE OF PROJECTIONS OF POTENTIAL ACTIVITY FROM THE PROPOSED ACTION

In order to describe the level of activity that could reasonably result from a proposed lease sale, MMS develops exploration and development scenarios of onshore and offshore activity. These scenarios provide a framework for detailed analyses of potential environmental and socioeconomic impacts of a proposed lease sale. Any potential effects on Louisiana's coastal zone would be the result of exploration, production, and transportation activities that may be undertaken as a result of the exploration and development of leases obtained in the lease sale. Assumptions are made about the kinds and levels of such activities. These assumptions are analyzed in the Multisale EIS and in this EA for Lease Sale 207 they are incorporated by reference. Projections of the number, probability, and size of accidental spills can be found in Chapter 4.3.1.5.1 of the Multisale EIS.

The MMS recently published a report that examined previous exploration and development activity scenarios (USDOI, MMS, 2007d). The MMS compared forecasted activity with the actual activity that has resulted in 14 WPA and 14 CPA lease sales between 1992 and 2005. The report shows that many lease sales contribute to the present level of OCS activity, and any single lease sale accounts for only a small percentage of the total OCS activities. Like other lease sales, Lease Sale 207 would contribute to maintaining the present level of OCS activity in the Gulf of Mexico. For example, in 2006 over half of the oil and gas production was the result of lease sales before 1992. An average lease in the WPA contributed 2 percent of oil production and 2 percent of gas production. For wells drilled annually, the contribution that resulted from lease sales before 1999 exceeded the contribution from leases in sales after 1999. For the installation of production structures in the WPA, the contribution of installations that resulted from lease sales after 1999 have greatly exceeded the contribution from lease sales that occurred before 1999. Exploration and development activity, including service-vessel trips, helicopter trips, and construction, that would result from Lease Sale 207 would replace activity resulting from existing leases that have reached or are near the end of their economic life.

4.1.1. Offshore Impact-Producing Factors and Scenario

The Multisale EIS discusses projections for activities associated with a typical proposed WPA lease sale. The estimated amounts of resources projected to be leased, discovered, developed, and produced as a result of proposed WPA Lease Sale 207 are 0.242-0.432 BBO and 1.644-2.647 Tcf of gas. **Table 1** provides a summary of the major scenario elements of proposed Lease Sale 207 based upon offshore, subarea water depths (**Figure 3**) and includes related impact-producing factors. Chapter 4.1.1 of the Multisale EIS describes the offshore infrastructure and activities (impact-producing factors) associated with the proposed lease sales and with the OCS Program that could potentially affect the biological, physical, and socioeconomic resources of the GOM.

The analyses of environmental and socioeconomic impacts in past EIS's (for example, the 2002-2007 Multisale EIS) were based on exploration and development activity scenarios that, in most cases, were overestimated. If the level of activity was overestimated, the environmental and socioeconomic impacts of a lease sale may have been overstated. Based on a recent analysis prepared by MMS, slightly over half of the time the actual activity fell below the lowest level of forecasted activity (USDOI, MMS, 2007d). When within the forecasted range, the majority of time the actual activity was at or near the low end of the forecasted range. In addition, a single lease sale accounts for only a small percentage of the total OCS activities.

The examination of previously forecasted activity did not include the proposed lease sales addressed in the Multisale EIS. In late 2002, MMS contracted with Innovation & Information Consultants, Inc. (IIC, Inc.) to develop a model that would estimate oil and gas exploration and discovery, development, and production activity in the Gulf of Mexico. The Exploration, Development, and Production (EDP) model was delivered to MMS in 2004. The activity scenario presented in the Multisale EIS was the first developed with the EDP model.

Table 1

Offshore Scenario Information Related to Proposed Lease Sale 207 over 40 Years

Activity	Offshore Subareas*							Total WPA**
	0-60	60-200	200-400	400-800	800-1600	1600-2400	>2400	
Wells Drilled								
Exploration and Delineation Wells	23-36	5-7	1	3-4	5-10	2-3	3-5	42-66
Development Wells	64-89	13-15	6-7	9-13	48-75	9-15	6-8	155-221
Oil Wells	3-5	2-2	1-2	6-8	29-45	6-9	3-5	51-76
Gas Wells	61-84	10-13	5-5	3-5	20-30	3-6	2-3	105-146
Workovers and Other Well Activities	392-539	77-91	35-42	56-77	294-455	56-91	35-49	945-1,344
Production Structures								
Installed	21-31	2	1	1	1-3	1-2	1	28-41
Removed Using Explosives	9-15	1	0	0	0	0	0	11-17
Total Removed	13-22	2	1	1	1-3	1	1	20-31
Method of Oil Transportation***								
Percent Piped	99%	100%	100%	100%	0% -50%	0% -100%	0 -100%	41% -> 99%
Percent Barged	1%	0%	0%	0%	0%	0%	0%	< 1%
Percent Tankered	0%	0%	0%	0%	0% -50%	0% -100%	0% -100%	0% -59%
Length of Installed Pipelines (km)#	60-420	NA	NA	NA	NA	NA	NA	130-760
Blowouts	1	0	0	0	0-1	0	0	1-2
Service-Vessel Trips (1,000 round trips)	23-33	3	1	16-17	18-51	16-33	16-17	94-155
Helicopter Operations (1,000 operations)	300-680	30-44	14-22	14-22	14-66	14-44	14-22	400-900

*See Figure 3.

**Subareas divided by water depth range in meters. Activity totals may not add up to the planning area total because of rounding.

***100% of gas is assumed to be piped.

#—Projected length of OCS pipelines does not include length in State waters.

NA means that information is not available.

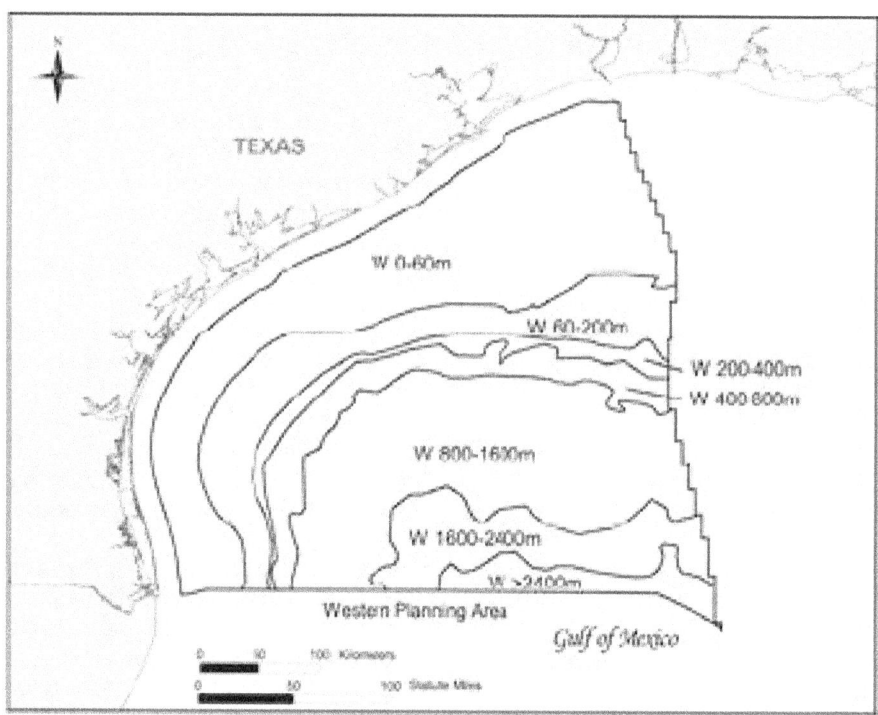

Figure 3.   Subareas of the Western Planning Area Zoned by Depth.

Documentation of the EDP model and its subcomponents can be found in Ashton et al. (2004). As stated in the model's documentation, the EDP model "incorporates actual historical data, and allows easy comparison between the actual historical data, and the future model years." As the model was developed, modifications were made so that the model more accurately portrayed historical precedent.

The EDP model relies on more factors than previous modeling methods (Upton and Ashton, 2005). Constraints include leasing policy, rig availability, and resource assessment. Inputs include prices, costs, field characteristics, reserve growth, and policy variables. The production function is based on historical production data by field size and location. Another improvement over previously used modeling methods is that the EDP model defines undiscovered resources by field instead of a Gulfwide undiscovered resource volume.

A recently published MMS study to estimate physical and economic performance measures to characterize lease sales and development in the Gulf of Mexico can be used to further refine the scenario presented in the Multisale EIS (Iledare and Kaiser, 2007). The average lag of exploration and production from leases issued from 1983 to 1999 increased by water depth and decreased over time as shown in the Tables 2 and 3. Due to variation by water depth, exploration and production activity is staggered over time taking on average 1.9-4.5 years after a lease sale before exploration begins and 3.4-8.3 years before first production. Therefore if activity as the result of a lease sale is assumed to be staggered over time, then the impacts and any strain on coastal infrastructure would also be staggered over time.

Table 2

Aggregate Average Lag in Months from Sales to First Spud for Leases Issued from 1983 to 1999

Water Depth	1983-1987	1985-1989	1990-1994	1995-1999
< 60m	29.3	27.8	25.8	22.9
60m - 200m	30.5	31.0	36.0	27.2
200m - 900m	40.4	46.4	42.9	30.0
>900m	84.9	93.3	84.2	53.6

Source: Iledare and Kaiser, 2007.

Table 3

Aggregate Average Lag in Months from Sales to First Production for Leases Issued from 1983 to 1999

Water Depth	1983-87	1985-1989	1990-1994	1995-1999
< 60m	59.0	53.2	49.5	41.1
60m - 200m	74.7	65.7	60.3	47.5
200m900m	128.1	123.0	70.2	54.1
>900m	180.6	176.9	105.9	99.6

Source: Iledare and Kaiser, 2007.

No new information has been found that necessitates a change to the offshore scenario presented in the Multisale EIS; therefore, the scenario still applies for proposed Lease Sale 207.

4.1.2. Coastal Impact-Producing Factors and Scenario

Chapter 4.1.2 of the Multisale EIS describes the onshore infrastructure and activities (impact-producing factors) associated with the proposed lease sales and with the OCS Program that could potentially affect the biological, physical, and socioeconomic resources of the GOM. Up to one new pipeline landfall and up to one new gas processing plant are projected as a result of an individual proposed lease sale. The MMS projected no other new coastal infrastructure as a result of a proposed lease sale.

The analyses of coastal infrastructure presented in the Multisale EIS and other previous EIS's and EA's concluded that no new solid waste facilities would be built as a result of a single lease sale or as a result of the OCS Program. Recent research further supports these past conclusions that existing solid-waste disposal infrastructure is adequate to support both existing and projected offshore oil and gas drilling and production needs (Dismukes et al., 2007).

The MMS projected the number of Federal OCS landfalls that may result from proposed lease sales in order to analyze the potential impacts on wetlands and other coastal habitats. In the Multisale EIS and other previous EIS's and EA's, MMS assumed that the majority of new Federal OCS pipelines would connect to the existing infrastructure in Federal and State waters and that very few would result in new pipeline landfalls. Therefore, MMS projected up to one pipeline landfall per lease sale; however, recent MMS analysis showed that even one landfall as a result of an individual lease sale may be unlikely (USDOI, MMS, 2007e). Although there will be some instances where new pipelines may need to be constructed, there is nothing to suggest any dramatic shifts in the trends in new Federal OCS landfalls given the current outlook for Gulf of Mexico development, particularly in coastal Louisiana (Dismukes, personal communication, 2007). While there are some opportunities for new pipeline landfalls from increased production activity, many of those will be limited due to a number of factors associated with basic pipeline economics.

Much of the coastal infrastructure presented in the Multisale EIS was from the *OCS-Related Infrastructure in the Gulf of Mexico Fact Book* (The Louis Berger Group, Inc., 2004). An update of the fact book is currently in progress. No new information has been found that necessitates a change to the onshore scenario presented in the Multisale EIS; therefore, the scenario still applies for proposed Lease Sale 207.

4.1.3. Hurricanes

Spills Resulting from Hurricanes

Chapter 4.1.3.4.4.2 of the Multisale EIS discusses the cause and volume of spills that resulted from the 2004-2005 hurricanes. Since the publication of the Multisale EIS, MMS has revised information and quantities of oil spillage resulting from damages caused by Hurricanes Katrina and Rita in 2005 (USDOI, MMS, 2007f). The following is a summary of the revisions.

As of July 2007, MMS has identified 154 spills of petroleum products of ≥1 barrel (bbl), totaling 17,077 bbl that were lost from platforms, rigs, and pipelines on the Federal OCS. This is an increase from MMS's January 2007 report that had identified 125 spills, totaling 16,302 bbl (USDOI, MMS, 2007g).

The July 2007 report also discussed spills of <1 bbl. Between October 2005 and June 2007, there were approximately 600 petroleum spills of <1 bbl on the Federal OCS related to the 2005 hurricanes reported to the National Response Center (NRC). These NRC reports totaled to <50 bbl and averaged approximately 3 gallons each in volume. These spills of <1 bbl dissipate quickly due to evaporation, dispersion by the winds and currents, and dilution by the ocean waters. Three gallons of crude oil can briefly create an oil sheen over an area the size of an acre (43,560 ft^2) or more on the ocean surface. These small releases generally do not cause identifiable environmental impacts out in the open ocean.

Unchanged from the earlier report, there were no accounts of environmental consequences resulting from spills from facilities:

- no spill contacts to the shoreline;

- no oiling of marine mammals, birds, or other wildlife;

- no large volumes of oil on the ocean surface to be collected or cleaned up; and

- no identified environmental impacts from any OCS spills from Hurricanes Katrina or Rita.

The final estimation of the total spillage associated with Hurricanes Katrina and Rita will not be complete until all operators have completed recovery efforts associated with the repair and/or have completed decommissioning of all the damaged structures. These activities will continue through 2008.

Damage to Offshore Infrastructure Resulting from Hurricanes

During the past few years, the Gulf Coast States and GOM oil and gas activities have been impacted by several major hurricanes. Chapter 3.3.5.7.3 of the Multisale EIS summarized the latest reports by MMS on the damage to the OCS-related platforms, rigs, and pipelines caused by Hurricane Ivan in 2004, and Hurricanes Katrina and Rita in 2005. In 2006, however, the only hurricane making landfall in the northern Gulf was Hurricane Humberto near Houston, Texas, on September 13, 2006. The 2007 hurricane season had no storm landfalls in the northern Gulf.

In preparation for the 2007 hurricane season, MMS announced operational and administrative improvements that had been implemented to prepare oil and gas infrastructure in the GOM for the possibility of hurricanes during the 2007 season (USDOI, MMS, 2007h). Both MMS and industry had to reassess what possible weather conditions could occur with a major hurricane moving through the GOM. The reassessment was done through American Petroleum Institute (API) committees in which MMS was an active participant. The committees revised and updated the best practices and standards using the new information that had been collected following the 2005 hurricanes.

Notices to Lessees

In addition to several NTL's that were specifically issued for the 2006 and 2007 hurricane seasons, MMS issued NTL 2007-G27 ("Assessment of Existing OCS Platforms and Related Structures for Hurricane Conditions") and NTL 2007-G26 ("Design of New OCS Platforms and Related Structures for Hurricane Conditions") to ensure that the assessment of existing and the design of new OCS platforms and related structures consider the specific environmental conditions, including hurricane metocean conditions, at the platform location as required by 30 CFR 250.900(a).

Hurricane and Tropical Storm Effects Reports (NTL 2007-G16)

The MMS issued NTL 2007-G16, "Hurricane and Tropical Storm Effects Reports," on May 14, 2007. The NTL provides clarification on using MMS's e-Well Permitting and Reporting System to report hurricane and tropical storm effects by specifying the information included in the various hurricane and tropical storm reports, updating contact information, and updating a regulatory citation. Under 30 CFR 250.192, operators must submit statistics to MMS regarding the evacuation of personnel and the curtailment of production because of hurricanes and tropical storms. The MMS has established the Facility Shut-in Report, three facility damage reports, and the Pollution Report to supplement and provide more detail about the required evacuation and production shut-in statistics. The MMS uses these data and information to work interactively with the U.S. Coast Guard (USCG) on rescue needs and to notify the news media and interested public entities that monitor shut-in production and hurricane and tropical storm damage. The MMS uses the data from the pollution report to identify environmental and manmade assets at risk, provide background data for natural resource damage assessments, assist the USCG in prioritization and coordination of oil-spill-response operations, and for status reports to public and private entities.

Pipeline Risers Subject to the Platform Verification Program (NTL 2007-G14)

The MMS issued NTL 2007-G14, "Pipeline Risers Subject to the Platform Verification Program," on May 7, 2007. The MMS has determined that new pipeline risers are subject to a separate verification process that necessitates the use of an independent Certified Verification Agent (CVA) specifically for the pipeline riser. These pipeline risers are a critical component of any floating platform proposal and must meet stringent requirements for design, fabrication, and installation. Accordingly, MMS has developed the guidelines for the pipeline riser verification process as part of the platform verification program. The CVA responsibilities include performance of an independent stress analysis, including extreme storm response for critical design conditions.

Contact with District Offices and the Pipeline Section Outside Regular Work Hours (NTL 2007-G12)

The MMS issued NTL 2007-G12, "Contact with District Offices and the Pipeline Section Outside Regular Work Hours," on April 4, 2007. The purpose of the NTL is to describe procedures that operators can use when contacting an MMS, GOM Region, District Office or the MMS, GOM Region, Pipeline Section outside of regular office hours. As required by 30 CFR 254.46(a), the National Response Center at (800) 424-8802 must immediately be notified if an offshore oil spill is observed.

4.2. ENVIRONMENTAL AND SOCIOECONOMIC RESOURCES

A detailed impact analysis of the routine, accidental, and cumulative impacts of a typical WPA lease sale, which is representative of proposed Lease Sale 207, on environmental and socioeconomic resources can be found in Chapters 4.2.1, 4.4, and 4.5 of the Multisale EIS, respectively. The following chapters provide a summary of these potential impacts of proposed Lease Sale 207 on each environmental and socioeconomic resource and the conclusions of the analyses. The cumulative analysis considers environmental and socioeconomic impacts that may result from the incremental impact of proposed Lease Sale 207 when added to all past, present, and reasonably foreseeable future human activities, including non-OCS activities, as well as all OCS activities (OCS Program).

New information discovered since publication of the Multisale EIS is also presented below. This information was evaluated to determine if reanalysis of the impacts of proposed Lease Sale 207 was necessary. No new information was found that would necessitate a reanalysis of the impacts of proposed Lease Sale 207 upon environmental or socioeconomic resources. The analyses and potential impacts detailed in the Multisale EIS apply for proposed Lease Sale 207. New information was found that further supports or elaborates on analyses or information presented in the Multisale EIS, but it does not change the conclusions of any of the analyses in the Multisale EIS.

4.2.1. Air Quality

The description of air quality in the Gulf of Mexico can be found in Chapter 3.1.1 of the Multisale EIS. A detailed impact analysis of the routine, accidental, and cumulative impacts of proposed Lease Sale 207 on air quality can be found in Chapters 4.2.1.1.1, 4.4.1, and 4.5.1 of the Multisale EIS, respectively. The following information is a summary of the impact analysis incorporated from the Multisale EIS. Figure 3-1 of the Multisale EIS presents the air quality status (i.e., ozone nonattainment) in the Gulf Coast as of September 2005. Figure 4 shows the current status of these coastal counties as of June 20, 2007 (USEPA, 2007b).

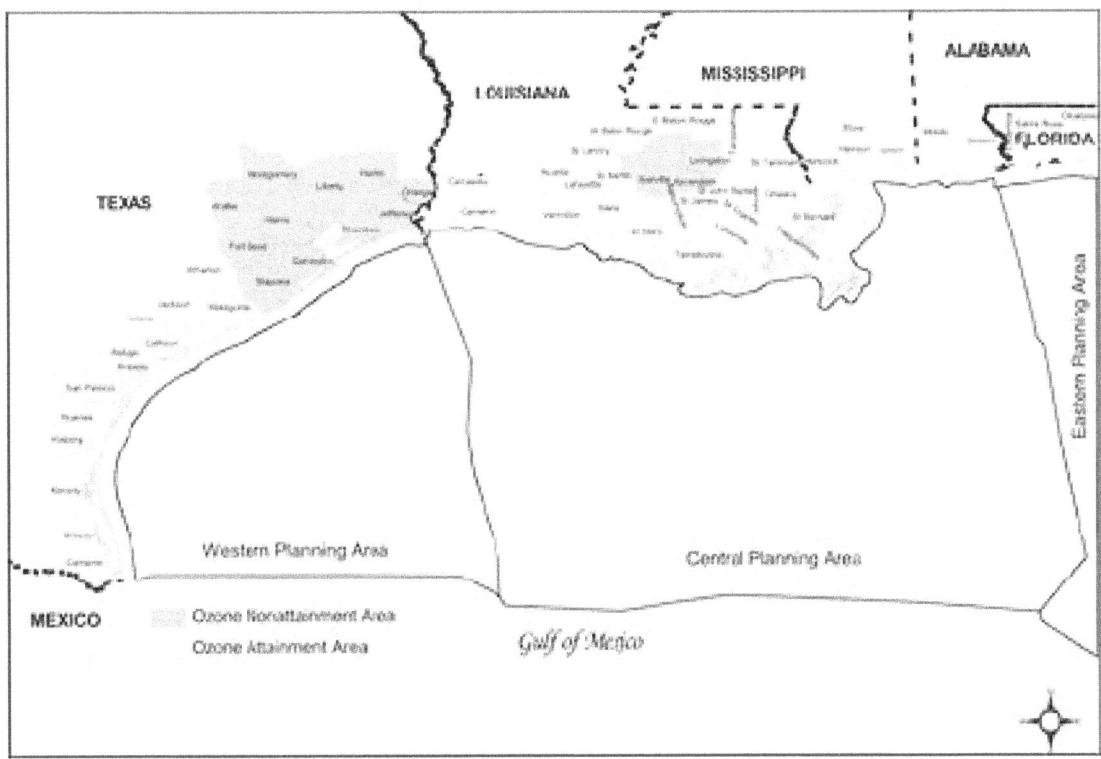

Figure 4.   Status of Ozone Attainment in the Coastal Counties and Parishes of the Central and Western
            Gulf of Mexico (USEPA, 2007b).

The following routine activities associated with proposed Lease Sale 207 would potentially affect air quality: platform construction and emplacement; platform operations; drilling activities; flaring; seismic-survey and support-vessel operations; pipeline laying and burial operations; evaporation of volatile petroleum hydrocarbons during transfers and from surface oil slicks; and fugitive emissions. Supporting materials and discussions are presented in the Multisale EIS in Chapters 3.1.1 (description of the coastal air quality status of the Gulf coastal area), 4.1.1.6 (air emissions), and 4.1.1.9 (hydrogen sulfide). The parameters of this analysis are emission rates, surface winds, atmospheric stability, and the mixing height.

Emissions of pollutants into the atmosphere from the routine activities associated with proposed Lease Sale 207 are projected to have minimal impacts on onshore air quality because of the prevailing atmospheric conditions, emission heights, emission rates, and the distance of these emissions from the coastline. Impacts from proposed Lease Sale 207 activities are expected to be well within the National Ambient Air Quality Standards (NAAQS).

Portions of the Gulf Coast have ozone levels that exceed the Federal air quality standard, but the cumulative contribution from proposed Lease Sale 207 is very small. Ozone levels are on a declining trend because of air pollution control measures that have been implemented by States. This downward trend is expected to continue as a result of local as well as nationwide air pollution control efforts. Proposed Lease Sale 207 would have only a small effect on ozone levels in ozone nonattainment areas and would not interfere with the States' schedule for compliance with the NAAQS.

Accidents involving high concentrations of H_2S could result in deaths as well as environmental damage. Other emissions of pollutants into the atmosphere from accidental events as a result of proposed Lease Sale 207 are not projected to have significant impacts on onshore air quality because of the prevailing atmospheric conditions, emissions height, emission rates, and the distance of these emissions from the coastline. These emissions are not expected to have concentrations that would change onshore air quality classifications.

Emissions of pollutants into the atmosphere from the activities associated with the cumulative scenario are not projected to have significant effects on onshore air quality because of the prevailing atmospheric conditions, emission rates and heights, and the resulting pollutant concentrations. Onshore impacts on air quality from emissions from cumulative OCS activities are estimated to be within Class II PSD allowable increments.

The Offshore and Coastal Dispersion modeling results show that increases in onshore annual average concentrations of NO_x, SO_2, and PM_{10} are estimated to be less than the maximum increases allowed in the PSD Class II areas.

The modeling results indicate that all concentrations are below the maximum allowable PSD increments except 24-hr SO_2 and annual NO_2 for the Class I area. The impacts from proposed Lease Sale 207 are well within the PSD Class I allowable increment. The incremental contribution of emissions resulting from proposed Lease Sale 207 (as analyzed in Chapter 4.2.1.1 in the Multisale EIS) to the cumulative impacts is not significant and is not expected to alter onshore air quality classifications.

The Gulf Coast has significant visibility impairment from anthropogenic emission sources. Area visibility would be expected to improve somewhat as a result of regional and national programs to reduce emissions. The cumulative contribution to visibility impairment from proposed Lease Sale 207 is also expected to remain very small.

The conclusions above only consider the impact on air quality from OCS sources. If the onshore sources are considered, there may be considerable adverse effects on ozone concentration and on visibility (see also the Final EIS on the proposed OCS Oil and Gas Leasing Program, 2007-2012; USDOI, MMS, 2007c). Thus, the OCS contribution to the air quality problem in the coastal areas is small, but total impact from onshore and offshore emissions may be significant to the ozone nonattainment areas in southeast Texas and the parishes near Baton Rouge, Louisiana.

The MMS is responsible for assessing the potential impacts of air pollutant emissions from offshore oil and gas exploration, development, and production sources in the OCS. This responsibility is driven by the OCS Lands Act, which directs the MMS to regulate OCS emission sources to assure that they do not significantly affect onshore air quality. The MMS air quality regulations are contained in 30 CFR 250.302 through 304. In particular, MMS is responsible for determining if air pollutant emissions from oil and natural gas platforms and other sources in the Gulf of Mexico influence the ozone attainment (and nonattainment) status of onshore areas. This responsibility was mandated by the Clean Air Act Amendments of 1990 (CAAA).

In addition, the CAAA requires MMS to coordinate air pollution control activities with USEPA. Thus, there will be a continuing need for emission inventories and modeling in the future, especially with the implementation of the 8-hour ozone standard. The future area of interest is not only Louisiana and Texas but it also includes Mississippi, Alabama, and Florida. Under provisions of the CAAA, the U.S. Environmental Protection Agency's (USEPA) Administrator, in consultation with the Secretary of the Interior and the Commandant of the Coast Guard, will establish the requirements to control air pollution in OCS areas of the Pacific, Atlantic, Arctic, and eastward of 87° 30' W. longitude in the Gulf of Mexico.

To assess the emissions of offshore oil and gas platforms and their associated emissions, MMS first conducted emission inventories in the GOM in the early 1990's, resulting in the Gulf of Mexico Air Quality Study (GMAQ) (Systems Applications International et al., 1995). To develop a base year 2000 inventory of criteria pollutant and greenhouse gas emissions for all OCS oil and gas production-related sources in the Gulf of Mexico, MMS collected activity data from platform operators during the year 2000 (Wilson et al., 2004). Inventory data has been collected for 2005 and is now being used (USDOI, MMS, 2007k). An emission inventory study has recently been awarded so that more inventory data will be collected for 2008.

Additionally, a 5-year meteorological database will be completed soon. This database will be used by industry and MMS in point-source modeling in plans analysis to ensure there are no significant impacts on onshore areas (Haney and Douglas, in preparation). The MMS is conducting an ongoing synthesis study (Haney and Douglas, ongoing) that will consolidate all MMS air quality studies, meteorological studies, and emissions studies into one database to determine links between parts. The USEPA has proposed a new ozone 8-hour standard and they will issue final standards by March 12, 2008 (USEPA, 2007a).

The MMS is coordinating with the University of Alabama, Huntsville (UAH) on the MMS's Satellite Data Assimilation project to test a newly developed, physically consistent, method for assimilating satellite temperatures into Mesoscale Model 5 (MM5) meteorological model preprocessors. Since the MM5 meteorological model is too complex and time consuming to test software algorithms, a one-dimensional model has been developed to quickly test the new formulation and isolate the results. The

UAH continues to coordinate with USEPA on the new algorithm development and model enhancements as the transition proceeds from MM5 to Weather Research and Forecast (WRF). The UAH is collaborating with NOAA/USEPA's Atmospheric Modeling Division to make this project's satellite data and assimilation techniques available to the air quality modeling community. The satellite assimilation technique will be implemented in the latest version of WRF and will likely result in meteorological improvements, which translate into air quality model improvements, resulting in better air quality model assessments of OCS impacts on adjacent onshore areas. The MMS's support of UAH research has resulted in one published technical article with two others in preparation. Likewise, MMS has funded the operating cost for two radar wind profilers to provide additional meteorological data to use in MM5, which in return will yield more accurate regional air quality modeling.

The MMS has reexamined the analysis for air quality presented in the Multisale EIS, based on the additional information presented above. No new significant information was discovered that would alter the impact conclusion for air quality presented in the Multisale EIS; therefore, a new analysis of the potential impacts of proposed Lease Sale 207 on air quality is not required. The analysis and potential impacts detailed in the Multisale EIS still apply for proposed Lease Sale 207.

4.2.2. Water Quality

A description of water quality in coastal and marine waters can be found in Chapter 3.1.2 of the Multisale EIS. An analysis of the routine, accidental, and cumulative impacts of proposed Lease Sale 207 on water quality can be found in Chapters 4.2.1.2, 4.4.2, and 4.5.2 of the Multisale EIS, respectively. The following information is a summary of the impact analysis incorporated from the Multisale EIS.

The primary impacting sources to water quality in coastal waters from routine operations are point-source and storm-water discharges from land-based support facilities, maintenance dredging of navigation canals, pipeline installations, and vessel discharges while in coastal waters. The impacts on coastal water quality from proposed Lease Sale 207 should be minimal as long as all existing regulatory requirements are met.

The primary impacting sources to marine water quality during exploratory activities are discharges of drilling fluids and cuttings. During installation activities, the primary impacting sources to water quality are sediment disturbance and turbidity. Impacting discharges during production activities include produced water and supply-vessel discharges. Regulations are in place to limit the levels of contaminants in these discharges. During platform removal, sediment disturbance, gaseous by-products of explosives, or abrasive grit from cutting are the impacting discharges. Impacts on marine waters from routine activities associated with proposed Lease Sale 207 should be minimal as long as regulatory requirements are followed.

Accidental events associated with proposed Lease Sale 207 that could impact water quality include spills of oil and refined hydrocarbons, spills of chemicals or drilling fluids, and collisions and loss of well control that result in spills. Water quality is altered and degraded by oil spills through the increase of petroleum hydrocarbons and their various transformation/degradation products in the water. The extent of impact from a spill depends on the behavior and fate of oil in the water column (e.g., movement of oil and rate and nature of weathering), which, in turn, depends on oceanographic and meteorological conditions at the time. Smaller spills (<1,000 bbl) are not expected to significantly impact water quality in marine and coastal waters. Larger spills, however, could impact water quality, especially in coastal waters. Chemical spills, the accidental release of synthetic-based fluids, and blowouts are expected to have temporary localized impacts on water quality.

Coastal water quality can be cumulatively impacted by inputs, which are transported through river inflows. These inputs include hydrocarbons, trace metals, sediment, and nutrients from human activities. Cumulative impacts on the water quality of the marine environment result from the addition of discharges from exploratory and production activities to a relatively pristine environment. The incremental contribution of proposed Lease Sale 207 to the cumulative impacts on marine water quality is not expected to be significant as long as all regulations are followed.

A search for the most recent information took place during preparation of this EA for Lease Sale 207. An Internet search for relevant scientific journal articles was conducted using a publicly available search engine. In addition, the websites for Federal and State agencies, and the Gulf of Mexico Alliance were reviewed for newly released information. The Gulf of Mexico Alliance, a partnership between the Gulf

States, was organized in 2005 as a collaborative means to solve regional problems to implement the U.S. Ocean Action Plan.

Although new research and ongoing monitoring information is continuously available from many sources about various water quality parameters in the Gulf of Mexico, the new information located was related to issues that have already been summarized in this EA; therefore, it was not incorporated (Ache, written communication, 2007; USEPA, 2007d-e; LADEQ, 2007a; Texas Commission on Environmental Quality, 2007).

In June 2007, USEPA issued the National Estuary Program Coastal Condition Report (USEPA, 2007f). This report was the third in a series of coastal environmental assessments. The first two reports covered all U.S. coastal waters, whereas the third report assessed just those estuaries that are part of the National Estuary Program. These include Mobile Bay, Barataria-Terrebonne Estuary, Galveston Bay, and Coastal Bend Bays and Estuaries (Corpus Christi Bay Estuary). A water quality rating was determined and Coastal Bend Bays, Barataria Terrebonne Estuary, and Mobile Bay were rated fair, but Galveston Bay was rated poor due to elevated dissolved phosphorus and higher turbidity.

The USEPA's National Pollutant Discharge Elimination System (NPDES) general permit for the Western Gulf of Mexico (GMG290000, which authorizes discharges to surface water during drilling and production) was reissued on October 1, 2007 (USEPA, 2007g). The USEPA was a cooperating agency on the Multisale EIS, and USEPA relied on the Multisale EIS in reissuing the permit. The reissued permit includes several more stringent limitations than its predecessors. It requires submittal of the sublethal effects on growth and reproduction from the produced-water toxicity testing. It also imposes the new cooling water intake structure requirements on new offshore facilities that intake more than 2 million gallons per day, of which at least 25 percent is used for cooling purposes (Wilson, personal communication, 2007).

The zone of hypoxia on the Louisiana-Texas shelf occurs seasonally from nutrient-laden waters discharged from the Mississippi and Atchafalaya Rivers. The boundary of the WPA is on the distal western edge of the hypoxic zone that was identified in 2002 (Rabalais et al., 2002) and is shown in **Figure 5**. The zone is defined by waters with lower than normal oxygen content caused by the decomposition of algae and plankton that bloom in nutrient-enriched water discharged from the rivers. The hypoxic conditions last until local wind-driven circulation sufficiently mixes the water. The Action Plan to understand and reduce hypoxia is reassessed every 5 years. As part of the 2006 reassessment, an independent panel, the Science Advisory Board (SAB) Hypoxia Panel, was convened, and in November 2007 a draft version of the 2008 Action Plan became available for public comment (USEPA, 2007h). The 2008 Action Plan increases the responsibilities of State and Federal bodies and acknowledges that the goal to reduce the size of the zone by 2015 may not be met.

In July 2007, a 1,750 mi^2 (4,532 km^2) dead zone was discovered in Texas coastal waters, extending as far as 10 mi (16 km) offshore from just south of Galveston Bay to Matagorda Bay. The zone was thought to be a temporary phenomenon, resulting from heavy rains in June and July and high discharge of nutrient-laden water from the Brazos River. The zone of oxygen-deficient bottom water was expected to gradually dissipate with decreasing discharge from the Brazos River (Associated Press, 2007).

The contribution of produced water to hypoxic conditions is minimal. The amount of oxygen-demanding pollutants in produced water was determined for produced water discharged into the hypoxic zone (Veil et al., 2005) as a requirement for the reissued NPDES general permit. Existing hypoxia models were used to analyze the potential incremental impacts on the hypoxia from produced-water discharges. The USEPA determined that the potential impact of the hypoxia from produced-water discharges was insignificant (USEPA, 2007e). In May 2007, a large area (20,000-21,000 km^2, 7,722-8,108 mi^2) was forecasted for the hypoxic zone (LUMCON, 2007a). During the mapping cruise of July 21-28, 2007, the hypoxic zone measured 20,500 km^2 (7,915 mi^2) (LUMCON, 2007b), which is within 10 percent of the maximum area measured in 2002.

The MMS has reexamined the analysis for water quality presented in the Multisale EIS, based on the additional information presented above. No new significant information was discovered that would alter the impact conclusion for water quality presented in the Multisale EIS; therefore, a new analysis of the potential impacts of proposed Lease Sale 207 on water quality is not required. The analysis and potential impacts detailed in the Multisale EIS still apply for proposed Lease Sale 207.

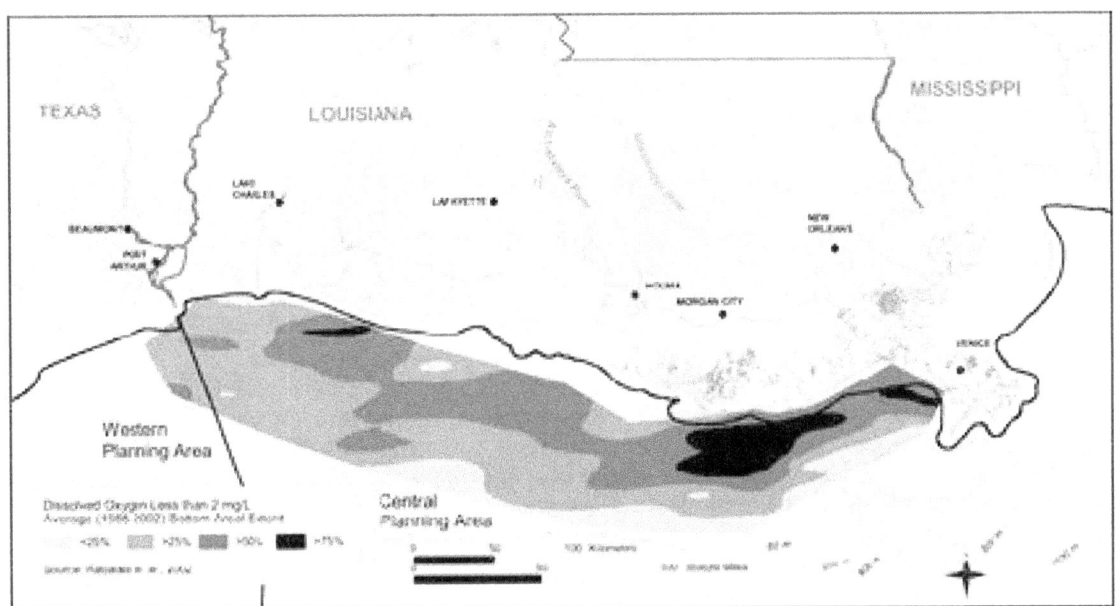

Figure 5.   Area of Hypoxia on the Outer Continental Shelf in 2002.

4.2.3.   Sensitive Coastal Environments

4.2.3.1.   *Coastal Barrier Beaches and Associated Dunes*

The description, physical location, and formative processes that create the various coastal beaches and barrier island complexes are described in Chapter 3.2.1.1 of the Multisale EIS. A description of integrated shoreline environments, the barrier islands, and the dune zones that comprise and delineate the various vegetated habitats along these mainland and barrier beaches can also be found in Chapter 3.2.1.1 of the Multisale EIS. A detailed impact analysis of the routine, accidental, and cumulative impacts of proposed Lease Sale 207 on barrier islands and coastal beaches can be found in Chapters 4.2.1.3.1, 4.4.3.1, and 4.5.3.1 of the Multisale EIS, respectively. The following information is a summary of the impact analysis incorporated from the Multisale EIS, and this analysis addresses the impacts of proposed Lease Sale 207.

A variety of activities required to support proposed Lease Sale 207 include pipeline emplacements, navigation channel use and dredging, and construction or continued use of oil and gas infrastructure. These activities are expected to be restricted to temporary and localized disturbances of the coastal barrier beaches and associated dunes. The 0-1 pipeline landfalls projected in support of proposed Lease Sale 207 are not expected to cause significant impacts on barrier beaches because of the use of non-intrusive installation methods. The projected 0-1 gas processing plant would not be expected to be constructed on barrier beaches. The use of existing facilities built inland may, through natural storm driven erosion and shoreline recession, be located in the barrier beach and dune zone and may contribute to the erosion there. Proposed Lease Sale 207 may contribute to the extended use of these facilities. No facilities are expected to be constructed on barrier beaches. Channel and inlet maintenance that is needed, as well as erosion protection works (jetties) required to assure access to the production and supply facilities, may contribute to minor and localized impacts on adjacent barrier beaches due to sediment deprivation. This would likely occur in the sediment starved coasts of Louisiana. Based on use, proposed Lease Sale 207 would account for a very small percentage of these impacts, which would occur whether proposed Lease Sale 207 is implemented or not. Strategic placement of dredged material from channel maintenance, channel deepening, or related actions can mitigate adverse impacts upon those localized areas. Proposed Lease Sale 207 is not expected to adversely alter barrier beach configurations significantly beyond existing, ongoing impacts in localized areas downdrift of artificially jettied and maintained channels.

No significant impacts on the physical shape and structure of the barrier beaches are expected as a result of accidental events associated with proposed Lease Sale 207. The primary accidental impacts that may be associated with proposed Lease Sale 207 would be the probability of offshore or coastal oil spills contacting the barrier or coastal beaches. The probabilities of proposed-action-related spills occurring in OCS waters and contacting various parishes and counties are provided in Chapter 4.3.1 of the Multisale EIS. The risk of offshore spills ≥1,000 bbl occurring and contacting barrier beaches within 10 days is discussed in Chapter 4.3.1.8 of the Multisale EIS. Generally, the coastal, deltaic parishes of Louisiana have the highest risk of being contacted by an offshore spill resulting from proposed Lease Sale 207; Plaquemines Parish has the highest probability at 10-15 percent. Should a slick from such a spill make landfall, the volume of oil remaining in the slick is expected to be small and its condition degraded. Coastal spills in offshore coastal waters or in the vicinity of Gulf tidal inlets present a greater potential risk to barrier beaches because of their close proximity. Inland spills that occur away from Gulf tidal inlets are generally not expected to significantly impact barrier beaches and dunes. The passage of two powerful hurricanes in 2005 (Katrina and Rita) resulted in changes in barrier island topography, lowering beach elevation and, therefore, potentially increasing the probability for beach oiling farther up the beach in some locations. Due to the now more gentle slopes and, in some cases, cuts into the mainland barrier beaches left by the storms, more of the transition zone between the water and beach ridge may be vulnerable to spills. Should a spill contact a barrier beach, oiling is expected to be light and sand removal during cleanup activities should be minimized. No significant impacts on the physical shape and structure of barrier beaches and associated dunes are expected to occur as a result of proposed Lease Sale 207.

Under the cumulative scenario, river channelization, sediment deprivation, tropical and extra-tropical storm activity, sea-level rise, and subsidence will continue to result in severe, rapid erosion of most shoreline landforms along the Louisiana coast. The barrier system of coastal Mississippi and Alabama is well supported on a coastal barrier platform of sand. The Texas coast has experienced landloss because of a decrease in the volume of sediment delivered to the coast caused by dams on coastal rivers, a natural decrease in sediment supply as a result of climatic changes during the past several thousand years, and subsidence along the coast. Louisiana is currently continuing to initiate ongoing, State- and federally-sponsored coastal programs and projects through the Coastal Wetlands, Planning, Protection and Restoration Act (CWPPRA), GOMESA, CIAP, and Louisiana Coastal Area (LCA) programs, along with the federally-funded CIAP initiatives being finalized and managed by MMS. All of these programs will cumulatively protect, build, restore, and enhance coastal ecosystems, and they will attempt to reduce coastal landloss in general and will include assistance in coastal and barrier beach rehabilitation or restoration. Beach stabilization projects that involve the construction of seawalls, groins, and jetties are considered by some coastal geomorphologists and engineers to accelerate coastal erosion (Pilkey and Dixon, 1996). Beneficial use of maintenance dredged materials could be required to mitigate some of these impacts.

The impacts of oil spills from both OCS and non-OCS sources to the sand-starved Louisiana coast should not result in long-term alteration if the beaches are cleaned using techniques that do not significantly remove sand from the beach or dunes. The region around Galveston, Texas, and the Chenier Plain of Louisiana have the greatest risk of sustaining impacts from oil-spill landfalls because of their very high concentrations of oil production within 31 mi (50 km) of the coast. The cleanup impacts of these spills could result in short-term (up to 2 years) adjustments in beach profiles and configurations as a result of sand removal and disturbance during cleanup operations. Some contact to lower areas of sand dunes would be expected. These contacts would not result in significant destabilization of the dunes. The long-term stressors to barrier beach communities caused by the physical effects and chemical toxicity of an oil spill may lead to decreased primary production, plant dieback, and hence further erosion. Under the cumulative scenario, new OCS-related and non-OCS pipeline landfalls are projected. These pipelines are expected to be installed using modern techniques, which cause little to no impacts on the barrier islands and beaches. Existing pipelines, in particular those parallel and landward of beaches and placed on barrier islands using older techniques that left canals or shore protection structures, have caused and will continue to cause barrier beaches to narrow and breach.

Coastal barrier beaches have experienced severe adverse cumulative impacts from natural processes and human activities. Natural processes are generally considered the major contributor to these impacts, whereas human activities cause both severe local impacts as well as the acceleration of natural processes that deteriorate coastal barriers. Human activities that have caused the greatest adverse impacts are river channelization and damming, pipeline canals, navigation channel stabilization and maintenance, and beach stabilization structures. The deterioration of Gulf barrier beaches is expected to continue in the future. Federal, State, and parish governments have made efforts over the last 10 years to slow the landward retreat of Louisiana's Gulf shorelines. Proposed Lease Sale 207 is not expected to adversely alter barrier beach configurations beyond existing, ongoing impacts in localized areas downdrift of artificially jettied and maintained channels. Proposed Lease Sale 207 may extend the life and presence of facilities in eroding areas, which would prolong erosion in those areas. Strategic placement of dredged material from channel maintenance, channel deepening, and related actions can mitigate adverse impacts upon those localized areas. Thus, the incremental contribution of proposed Lease Sale 207 to the cumulative impacts on coastal barrier beaches and dunes is expected to be very small.

A search was conducted for new information published since completion of the Multisale EIS. Various Internet sources were examined or revisited to determine any new information regarding barrier islands (FDEP, 2005 and 2007; Leadon, 2004; TGLO, 2007; USDOI, GS, 2006 and 2007a; White et al., 2005 and 2007). No new information was discovered from these information sources. A web search of available literature and agency Internet sites and personal interviews with various Federal and State agency researchers and mangers responsible for these coastal resources was conducted. The search found no additional information pertaining to Louisiana or Texas. The Texas Bureau of Economic Geology confirmed no further studies had been initiated by the State of Texas post-Rita (Tremplay, personal communication, 2007). Prior to Hurricane Rita, the Texas Bureau of Economic Geology had conducted a series of studies on the barrier islands, which is comprised of five different reports. The bureau is currently preparing a report on the Upper Strand Plain near Clam Lake and Padre Island. These studies are in the formative stages and drafts have not been released. Aerial photography of the flooded Texas coastal area following Hurricane Rita was examined, and previously flooded sites were visited post-Rita. Based on these observations, the majority of the flooded marshes are naturally reestablishing themselves and the sediment distribution along the barrier island fringe seems to appear stable.

In addition, The MMS has reexamined the analysis for coastal beaches and barrier island complexes presented in the Multisale EIS, based on the additional information presented above. While there was some refinement of post-storm data and working drafts of various storm impacts, no new significant information was discovered that would alter the impact conclusion for coastal beaches and barrier island complexes presented in the Multisale EIS; therefore, a new analysis of the potential impacts of proposed Lease Sale 207 on coastal beaches and barrier island complexes is not required. The analysis and potential impacts detailed in the Multisale EIS still apply for proposed Lease Sale 207.

4.2.3.2. Wetlands

A detailed description of coastal wetlands can be found in Chapter 3.2.1.2 of the Multisale EIS. A detailed impact analysis of the routine, accidental, and cumulative impacts of proposed Lease Sale 207 on coastal wetlands can be found in Chapters 4.2.1.3.2, 4.4.3.2, and 4.5.3.2 of the Multisale EIS, respectively. The following information is a summary of the impact analysis incorporated from the Multisale EIS. A detailed explanation of the routine and accidental impact-producing factors can be found in Chapters 4.1 and 4.3 of the Multisale EIS, respectively.

The primary impacts resulting from routine activities associated with proposed Lease Sale 207 that could affect wetlands and marshes include pipeline emplacement, construction and maintenance, navigation channel use (vessel traffic), maintenance dredging, disposal of OCS-related wastes, and the use and construction of support infrastructure in these coastal areas. Other potential impacts that are indirectly associated with OCS oil and gas activities are wake erosion resulting from navigational traffic, levee construction that prevents necessary sedimentary processes, saltwater intrusion that changes the hydrology leading to unfavorable conditions for wetland vegetation and vulnerability to storm damage from eroded wetlands. Simultaneously with man-made influences there are natural causes of subsidence that contribute to wetland loss. Compaction and dewatering of deltaic mud lead to subsidence. Likewise, down-to-the-basin faulting (listric) is a characteristic of sediment loading for deltaic wedges such as the modern Mississippi Delta system (Dokka et al., 2006).

Wetland loss rates in coastal Louisiana are well documented to have been as high as 10,878 ha/yr (42 mi²/yr) during the late 1960's. Studies have shown that the landloss rate in coastal Louisiana for the period 1972-1990 slowed to between an estimated 6,475 ha/yr (25 mi²/yr) (Louisiana Coastal Wetlands Conservation and Restoration Task Force, 1993) and 9,072 ha/yr (35 mi²/yr) (USDOI, GS, 1988). It was estimated in 2000 that coastal Louisiana would continue to lose land at a rate of approximately 2,672 ha/yr (10 mi²/yr) over the next 50 years. Barras et al (2003) estimated that a net loss of 132,794 ha

(512 mi^2) may occur by 2050, which is almost 10 percent of Louisiana's remaining coastal wetlands. Further, a recent report by the Government Accountability Office (2007) cites a projected landloss of $17 \text{ mi}^2/\text{yr}$ over the next 50 years. In 2005 Hurricanes Katrina and Rita caused 217 mi^2 (562 km^2) of land change, primarily wetland conversion to open water (Barras, 2006). The already eroded Louisiana barrier islands were significantly damaged by Hurricanes Katrina and Rita, thus further lowering the protection afforded the mainland marshes and beaches from storm surge or oil spills that these barrier features previously provided.

Based on the analysis of the latest satellite imagery (Barras, 2007; Barras, in press), approximately 82 mi^2 (212 km^2) of new water were in areas primarily impacted by Hurricane Katrina (Mississippi River Delta Basin, Breton Sound Basin, Pontchartrain Basin, and Pearl River Basin), whereas 99 mi^2 (256 km^2) were in areas primarily impacted by Hurricane Rita (Calcasieu/Sabine Basin, Mermentau Basin, Teche/Vermilion Basin, Atchafalaya Basin, and Terrebonne Basin). Barataria Basin contained new water areas caused by both hurricanes, resulting in some 18 mi^2 (46.6 km^2) of new water areas. The fresh marsh and intermediate marsh communities' land areas decreased by 122 mi^2 (316 km^2) and 90 mi^2 (233.1 km^2), respectively, and the brackish marsh and saline marsh communities' land areas decreased by 33 mi^2 (85.5 km^2) and 28 mi^2 (72.5 km^2), respectively. These new water areas represent landlosses caused by the direct removal of wetlands. These areas also indicate transitory changes in water area caused by remnant flooding, removal of aquatic vegetation, scouring of marsh vegetation, and water-level variation attributed to normal tidal and meteorological variation between satellite images. Barras (2007) noted permanent losses cannot be estimated until several growing seasons have passed and the transitory impacts of the hurricanes are minimized. It is, however, too early to estimate the actual overall marsh loss.

Effects of routine activities on coastal wetlands associated with proposed Lease Sale 207 are expected to be low. The loss of 0-8 ha (0-20 ac) of wetlands habitat is estimated as a result of 0-2 km (0-1.2 mi) of new onshore pipelines projected as a result of proposed Lease Sale 207. Maintenance dredging of navigation channels and canals is expected to occur with minimal impacts; proposed Lease Sale 207 is expected to contribute minimally to the need for this dredging. Alternative, dredged-material disposal methods can be used to enhance and create coastal wetlands. Vessel traffic associated with a proposed action is expected to contribute minimally to the erosion and widening of navigation channels and canals. The already eroded Louisiana barrier island chain was damaged significantly by Hurricanes Katrina and Rita, thus further lowering the protection afforded the mainland marshes and beaches from oil spills that these barrier features previously provided. Breton Island, one of the islands comprising the hard-hit Chandeleur barrier island chain, lost approximately 50 percent of its landmass (Hall, 2006). Overall, impacts from these sources are expected to be low and could be further reduced through mitigation, such as horizontal, directional (trenchless) drilling techniques to avoid damages to these sensitive habitats. Secondary impacts on wetlands would be primarily from vessel traffic corridors and will continue to cause approximately 0.57-0.72 ha (1.40-1.77 ac) of landloss per year.

The primary concern for potential impact from accidental activities associated with proposed Lease Sale 207 is related to oil spills. While there is a concern for offshore oil spills resulting from proposed Lease Sale 207, they are not expected to damage significantly wetlands along the Gulf Coast. If an inland oil spill related to proposed Lease Sale 207 occurs, however, some impact on wetland habitat would be expected. Although the impact may occur generally over coastal regions, the impact has the highest probability of occurring in and around Plaquemines and St. Bernard Parishes, Louisiana. Impacts on wetland habitats from an oil spill associated with activities related to Lease Sale 207 would be expected to be low and temporary. Although the probability of occurrence is low, the greatest threat to wetland habitat is from an inland spill resulting from a vessel accident or pipeline rupture. While a resulting slick may cause minor impacts on wetland habitat and surrounding seagrass communities, the equipment and personnel used to clean up a slick over the impacted area may generate the greatest impacts on the area. Associated foot traffic may work oil farther into the sediment than would otherwise occur. Close monitoring and restrictions on the use of bottom-disturbing equipment would be needed to avoid or minimize those impacts.

Concerns were raised related to the potential impact of oil spills on the marine and coastal environments, specifically regarding the potential effects of oil spills on tourism, emergency response capabilities, spill prevention, effect of winds and currents on the transport of oil spills, accidental discharges from both deepwater blowouts and pipeline ruptures, and oil spills resulting from past and future hurricanes. The fate and behavior of oil spills, availability and adequacy of oil-spill containment and cleanup technologies, oil-spill cleanup strategies, impacts of various oil-spill cleanup methods, effects of weathering on oil spills, toxicological effects of fresh and weathered oil, air pollution associated with spilled oil, and short-term and long-term impacts of oil on wetlands are additional accidental concerns. Offshore oil spills resulting from proposed Lease Sale 207 are not expected to damage significantly any wetlands along the Gulf Coast. However, if an inland oil spill related to proposed Lease Sale 207 occurs, some impact on wetland habitat would be expected.

The cumulative analysis in the Multisale EIS considers the effects of impact-producing factors related to past WPA lease sales, the present proposed Lease Sale 207, and reasonably foreseeable lease sale programs in the WPA. Cumulative impacts attributed to OCS activity co-occur with State oil and gas activities, other governmental and private projects and activities, and pertinent natural processes and events that may occur that adversely affect wetlands. As a result of these activities and processes, several impact-producing factors discussed in Chapter 4.5.3.2 of the Multisale EIS will contribute to impacts on wetlands and associated habitat during the life of proposed Lease Sale 207.

The cumulative effects of human and natural activities in the coastal area have severely degraded the natural process of delta-building and sediment replenishment and have shifted the coastal area from a condition of net land building to one of net landloss (USACOE, 2004). There is increasing new evidence of the importance of the effect of sea-level rise (or marsh subsidence) as it relates to the loss of marsh or changes in marsh types and plant diversity (Spalding and Hester, 2007). Spalding and Hester showed that the very structure of coastal wetlands will likely be altered by sea-level rise, as community shifts will be governed by the responses of individual species to new environmental conditions.

Subsidence rates may slow as a result of oil and gas depletion in onshore and nearshore areas that are producing. The magnitude of relative sea level rise caused by global warming as a contributor to wetland loss is uncertain. Relative sea level rise in any specific area takes into account that either the land sinks or the sea rises. In either case there would be a relative sea level rise. Estimates of magnitude for absolute sea level rise vary with the model used to project climatic scenarios into the future. The Intergovernmental Panel on Climate Change, Summary for Policymakers, states that since 1993 global sea level rise has taken place at a rate of 3.1 [2.4 to 3.8]mm/yr, with contributions from thermal expansion of ocean water, melting glaciers and ice caps, and the polar ice sheets (IPCC, 2007; page 1). Simply projecting this rate over the next 40 years, which may be a valid projection or not, and the cumulative effect of global sea level rise in the Gulf of Mexico could be a rise of 12.4 cm. (4.8 in). Sea level rise is likely to be a contributor to wetland loss over the next 40 years, however, the total acres lost attributed only to sea level rise is unknown because multiple contributors occurring simultaneously affect the number of total acres likely to be lost in Louisiana. Coastal restoration of barrier islands and headland areas and sediment replenishment projects may slightly mitigate the effects of subsidence and hurricane storm surge on wetland loss over the next 40 years.

The effects of pipelines, canal dredging, navigation activities, and oil spills on wetlands are described in Chapters 4.2.1.1.3.2, 4.4.3.2, and 4.5.3.2 of the Multisale EIS. Subsidence of wetlands is discussed in more detail in Chapter 4.1.3.3.1 of the Multisale EIS. Impacts from residential, commercial, and agricultural and silvicultural (forest expansion) developments are expected to continue in coastal regions around the Gulf. Existing regulations and development permitting procedures indicate that development-related wetland loss may be slowed and that very few new onshore OCS facilities, other than pipelines, will be constructed in wetlands. Impacts from State onshore oil and gas activities are expected to occur as a result of dredging for new canals, maintenance and usage of existing rig access canals and drill slips, and preparation of new well sites. Locally, subsidence may be due to the extraction of large volumes of oil and gas from subsurface reservoirs, although subsidence associated with this factor seems to have slowed greatly over the last three decades as the reservoirs are depleted. Indirect impacts from dredging new canals for State onshore oil and gas development (Chapter 4.1.3.3.3 of the Multisale EIS) and from maintenance of the existing canal network is expected to continue. Maintenance dredging of the OCS-related navigation channels displaces approximately 492,082,500 m^3 (643,619,611 yd^3) of sediment per 35 years, of which 10 percent is attributed to the OCS Program. Federally maintained, non-OCS-related navigation channels are estimated to account for another estimated 36,576,500 m^3 (47,840,256 yd^3) of dredged material. Maintenance dredging of inshore, well-access canals is estimated to result in the displacement of another 5,014,300 m^3 (6,558,457 yd^3) of materials. Insignificant adverse impacts upon wetlands from maintenance dredging are expected because the large majority of the material would be disposed upon existing disposal areas. Alternative, dredged-material disposal methods can be used to enhance and create coastal wetlands. Depending upon the regions and soils through which they were dredged, secondary adverse impacts of canals may be more locally significant than direct impacts. Additional wetland losses generated by the secondary impacts of saltwater intrusion, flank subsidence, freshwater-reservoir reduction, and deeper tidal penetration have not been calculated due to a lack of quantitative documentation. The MMS has initiated a study to document and develop data concerning such losses.

A variety of mitigation efforts are initiated to protect against direct and indirect wetland loss. The nonmaintenance of mitigation structures that reduce canal construction impacts can have substantial impacts upon wetlands. These localized impacts are expected to continue. Various estimates of the total, relative direct and indirect impacts of pipeline and navigation canals on wetland loss vary enormously. They range from a low of 9 percent (Britsch and Dunbar 1993) to 33 percent (Penland et al., 2001a and b) to estimates of greater than 50 percent (Turner et al., 1982; Bass and Turner, 1997; Scaife et al., 1983). A panel review of scientific evidence suggests that wetland losses directly attributable to all human activities account for less than 12 percent of the total wetland loss experienced since 1930 and approximately 29 percent of the total losses between 1955 and 1978 (Boesch et al., 1994). Of these direct losses, 33 percent are attributed to canal and spoil bank creation (10% of overall wetland loss). In Louisiana, deepening Fourchon Channel to accommodate larger, OCS-related service vessels has occurred within a saline marsh environment and will afford the opportunity for the creation of wetlands with the dredged materials. Also, deepening the Corpus Christi and Houston Ship Channels is non-OCS related and should also afford the opportunity to create wetlands with dredged material. A variety of non-OCS-related pressures are generating a need to expand ports on the Mississippi Gulf Coast.

Based on preliminary historic landloss results from the MMS/USGS National Wetlands Research Center current coastal pipeline impacts study for the Louisiana area, the predicted landloss from the estimated 64-94 km (40-58 mi) of new OCS pipeline construction ranges from approximately 256-376 ha (633-929 ac) total over the 40-year analysis period. This estimate does not take into account the current regulatory programs, modern construction techniques and mitigations, or any new techniques that might be developed in the future. The modern construction techniques and mitigation measures result in zero (0) to negligible impacts on wetland habitats.

The current MMS/USGS pipeline study is continuing to develop models that will aid in quantifying habitat loss associated with OCS activities. Proposed Lease Sale 207 represents about 3-4 percent of the OCS impacts that will occur during the period 2007-2046. The cumulative effects of human and natural activities in the coastal area have severely degraded the deltaic processes and shifted the coastal area from a condition of net land building to one of net landloss. Deltaic Louisiana is expected to continue to experience the greatest loss of wetland habitat. Wetland loss is also expected to continue in other Gulf States, including Texas, but at slower rates. The loss of 0-8 ha (0-20 ac) of wetlands habitat is estimated as a result of 0-2 km (0-1.2 mi) of new onshore pipelines projected as a result of proposed Lease Sale 207. Secondary impacts from proposed Lease Sale 207 to wetlands would be primarily from vessel traffic corridors and will continue to cause approximately 2.25-3.61 ac/yr of landloss for proposed Lease Sale 207. However, effective mitigation and construction techniques have been and would be used to prevent or minimize landloss.

The Government Accountability Office (2007) recently reviewed the range of wetlands restoration and shoreline stabilization techniques and methods that are available to retard landloss in Louisiana. In addition, the State of Louisiana has made provision for wetlands protection and restoration part of the States' plan for hurricane protection. The Louisiana State legislature established the Coastal Protection and Restoration Authority (CPRA) and charged it with coordinating the efforts of local, State, and Federal agencies to achieve long-term and comprehensive coastal protection and restoration that integrates flood control and wetland restoration. The following four objectives were defined for the plan: reduce the risk to economic assets; restore sustainability to the coastal ecosystem; maintain a diverse array of habitats for fish and wildlife; and sustain Louisiana's unique heritage and culture. The Final Master Plan (State of Louisiana, CPRA, 2007) was submitted to the Louisiana legislature on April 30, 2007, and was approved on May 30, 2007.

A search of Internet information sources (Bernier et al., 2006; Clark and LaGrone, 2006; FDEP, 2005 and 2007; USDOI, GS, 2007b-e), as well as an interview with a person from USGS (Cahoon, personal communication, 2007), was conducted to determine the availability of recent information. Various Internet sources were examined to assess recent information regarding wetland loss or potential new threats to coastal wetlands that may be pertinent to the WPA. The search revealed a recent study indicating the very structure of coastal wetlands will likely be altered by sea-level rise, as community shifts will be governed by the responses of individual species to new environmental conditions (Spalding and Hester, 2007). While this information is not new, the study did explore, through the use of controlled experiments, how the variance in flooding regime, salinities, and the particular plant species involved may evolve in different coastal environments than presently exist. Other findings related to changes in State-mandated coastal policies addressing wetland protection, restoration, preservation, and development. John Barras with the USGS Wetland Resources Center noted that, while the current wetland loss numbers cited in the Multisale EIS have not changed significantly, marsh recovery (or land gain) varies from location to location.

The MMS has reexamined the analysis for wetlands presented in the Multisale EIS, based on the additional information presented above. No new significant information was discovered that would alter the impact conclusion for wetlands presented in the Multisale EIS; therefore, a new analysis of the potential impacts of proposed Lease Sale 207 on wetlands is not required. The analysis and potential impacts detailed in the Multisale EIS still apply for proposed Lease Sale 207.

4.2.3.3. *Seagrass Communities*

The description of the biology and distribution of seagrass can be found in Chapter 3.2.1.3 of the Multisale EIS. A detailed impact analysis of the routine, accidental, and cumulative impacts of proposed Lease Sale 207 on seagrass can be found in Chapters 4.2.1.3.3, 4.4.3.3, and 4.5.3.3 of the Multisale EIS, respectively. The following information is a summary of the impact analysis incorporated from the Multisale EIS.

The routine activities associated with proposed Lease Sale 207 that could adversely affect seagrass communities include construction of pipelines, canals, navigation channels, and shore facilities; maintenance dredging; vessel traffic (propeller scars, etc.); and oil spills, spill-response, and cleanup activities. Environmental permit requirements for locating pipelines will result in very minimal impact on seagrass if any new pipeline runs to shore due to proposed Lease Sale 207. Impacts from routine activities resulting from proposed Lease Sale 207 are expected to have negligible effects on seagrass communities.

Pipeline construction in coastal waters would temporarily elevate turbidity in nearby submerged vegetation beds, depending upon currents. If constructed, the pipeline landfall would temporarily elevate turbidity in submerged vegetation beds near the pipeline routes. The COE and State permit requirements are expected to require pipeline routes that avoid beds of high-salinity, submerged vegetation and to reduce turbidity impacts to within tolerable limits. Hence, impacts on submerged vegetation by pipeline installation are projected to be very small and short term.

After bottom sediments are disturbed by pipeline installation, they will be generally more easily suspended by storms than before the disturbance. Due to tidal flushing increased turbidity in estuaries is projected to be below significant levels.

Dredging generates the greatest overall risk to submerged vegetation, and hurricanes cause direct damage to seagrass beds, which may fail to recover in the presence of cumulative stresses. Maintenance dredging will not have a significant impact on existing seagrass habitat given that no new channels are expected to be dredged as a result of proposed Lease Sale 207. Increased dredging is expected only in areas that do not support seagrass beds.

Vessel traffic will generally only pose a risk to seagrass when nearshore. Beds of submerged vegetation within a navigation channel's area of influence will have already adjusted their bed configurations in response to turbidity generated there. Very little, if any, damage would then occur as a result of typical channel traffic. Generally, propeller wash will not resuspend sediments in navigation channels beyond pre-project conditions.

Depending upon the submerged plant species involved, narrow prop scars in dense portions of the beds will take 1-7 years to recover. Scars through sparser areas will take 10 years or more to recover. The recovery period increases with the width of the scar. Extensive damage to a broad area or damage to an already stressed area may never recover (Sargent et al., 1995; Durako et al., 1992).

Most seagrass communities are located behind barrier islands. Because of the location of most seagrass communities, inshore oil spills pose the most severe threat. Such spills may result from either vessel collisions that release fuel and lubricants or from pipelines that rupture. If an oil slick settles into a protective embayment where seagrass beds are found, shading may cause reduced chlorophyll production and thinning of leaf density. Increased water turbulence due to storms or vessel traffic can break apart the surface sheen and disperse some oil into the water column, potentially causing some dieback of leaves for one growing season. It may take as much as 5-10 years of community succession before faunal composition resembles pre-impact conditions.

A search was conducted for new information published since completion of the Multisale EIS. Various Internet sources were examined to determine any recent information regarding seagrass. Sources investigated include the USGS National Wetlands Research Center, the USGS Gulf of Mexico Integrated Science Data Information Management System, Gulf of Mexico Alliance workshops in spring of 2007, Florida Department of Environmental Protection, USEPA, and coastal universities. Other sites were checked using general Internet searches based on major themes. New information was identified from these sources and is discussed below.

Workshops held by the Gulf of Mexico Alliance in the spring of 2007 revealed new studies of seagrass on the Texas coast. Hardegree (2007) highlighted declines in seagrass in Christmas Bay and the Lower Laguna Madre. He also analyzed propeller scarring, recovery, and regulation.

The MMS has reexamined the analysis for seagrass presented in the Multisale EIS, based on the additional information presented above. This new information supports previous assessments. No new significant information was discovered that would alter the impact conclusion for seagrass presented in the Multisale EIS; therefore, a new analysis of the potential impacts of proposed Lease Sale 207 on seagrass is not required. The analysis and potential impacts detailed in the Multisale EIS still apply for proposed Lease Sale 207.

4.2.4. Sensitive Offshore Benthic Resources

4.2.4.1. Continental Shelf Benthic Resources

4.2.4.1.1. Topographic Features

The description of the biology of topographic features can be found in Chapter 3.2.2.1.2 of the Multisale EIS. A detailed impact analysis of the routine, accidental, and cumulative impacts of proposed Lease Sale 207 on topographic features can be found in Chapters 4.2.1.4.1.1, 4.4.4.1.2, and 4.5.4.1.2 of the Multisale EIS, respectively. A description of the Topographic Features Stipulation governing oil and gas activities near these features can be found in Chapter 2.4.1.3.1 of the Multisale EIS. The following information is a summary of the impact analysis incorporated from the Multisale EIS.

Potential OCS-related impacts include the anchoring of vessels, emplacement of oil and gas structures, operational discharges (drilling mud and cuttings, and produced waters), blowouts, oil spills, and removal of structures. Activities causing mechanical disturbance or direct contact represent the greatest threat to the topographic features. This would, however, be prevented by the continued application of the Topographic Features Stipulation. Named topographic features from the northern Gulf of Mexico are shown in **Figure 6**.

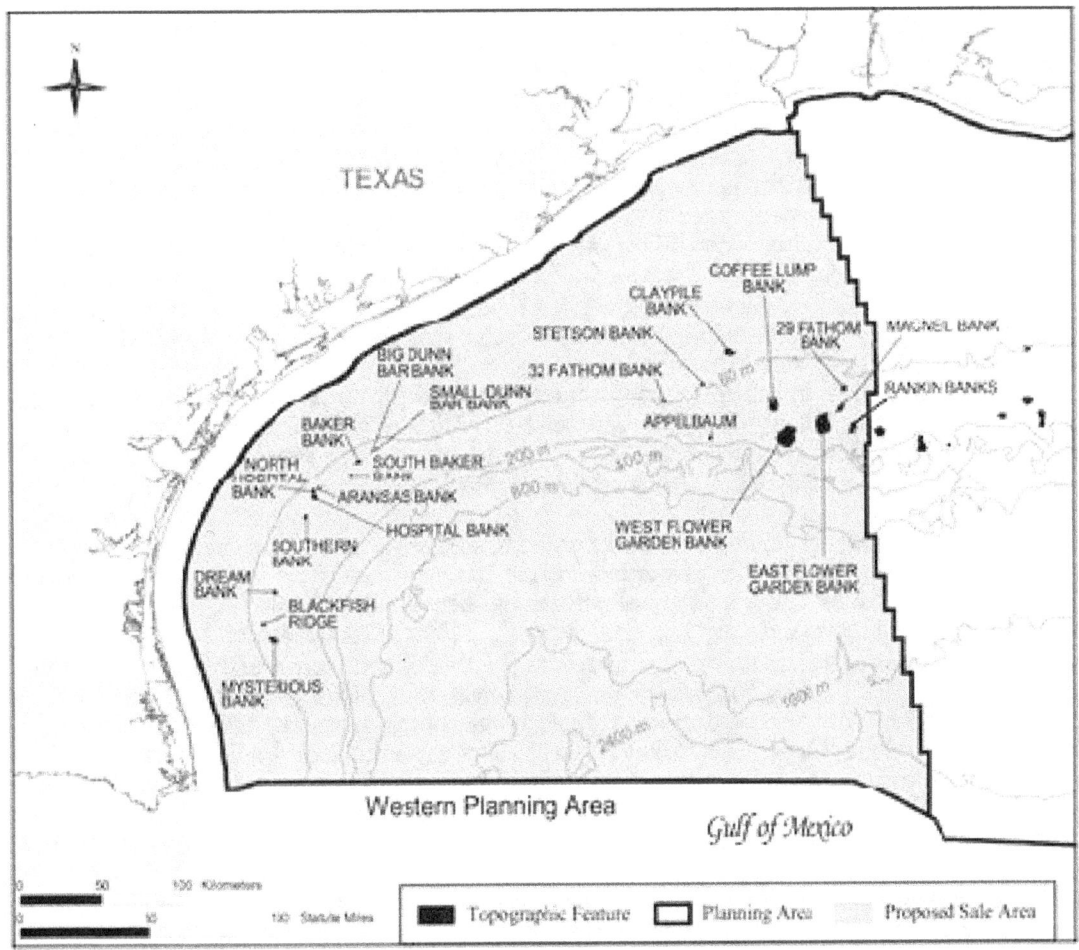

Figure 6. Named Topographic Features in the Northern Gulf of Mexico.

Non-OCS activities are thought to have the greatest potential of impacting the topographic features, particularly those that could mechanically disrupt the bottom (such as anchoring and treasure-hunting activities). Natural events such as hurricanes or the collapse of the tops of the topographic features (through dissolution of the underlying salt structure) could cause severe impacts. Impacts from scuba diving, fishing, ocean dumping, and discharges or spills from tankering of imported oil are likely to have little or no impact on the topographic features because these activities are either controlled, prohibited, or take place on the surface; therefore, they would not pose a hazard to the Flower Gardens National Marine Sanctuary and other topographic features.

It is assumed that a resuspension of sediments or a subsurface oil spill following a blowout could reach the biota of a topographic feature. If this were to occur, the impacts would be primarily sublethal with the disruption or impairment of a few elements at the local scale, but no interference to the general system performance would occur. Oil spills can cause damage to benthic organisms when the oil contacts organisms. In the unlikely event that oil from a subsurface spill would reach the biota of a topographic feature, the effects would be primarily sublethal for corals and much of the other fully developed biota. It is anticipated that potential recovery for such an event would occur within a period of 2 years (USDOC, NOAA, Office of Response and Restoration, 2007; Shigenaka, 2001; Rice et al., 1983). In the highly unlikely event that oil from a subsurface spill reached an area containing coral cover (e.g., Flower Garden Banks and Stetson Bank) in lethal concentrations, the impacted area would be small, but its recovery could take in excess of 10 years. However, due to the application of the proposed Topographic Features

Stipulation, blowouts would not occur in the immediate vicinity of the topographic features and associated biota. Therefore, there would be little impact on the features.

The incremental contribution of proposed Lease Sale 207 (as analyzed in Chapter 4.2.1.1.4.1.1 of the Multisale EIS) to the cumulative impact is negligible because of the implementation of the Topographic Features Stipulation limits mechanical impacts and operational discharges. Furthermore, there is a low probability and low risk of accidental OCS-related events such as blowouts and oil spills occurring in the immediate vicinity of a topographic feature.

A search was conducted for new information published since completion of the Multisale EIS. Various Internet sources were examined to identify any recent information regarding topographic features. Sources investigated include USGS National Wetlands Research Center, USGS Gulf of Mexico Integrated Science Data Management System, Gulf of Mexico Alliance workshops held in spring 2007, NOAA, USEPA, and coastal universities. Other sites were found through general Internet searches.

One ongoing study reports some preliminary results that indicate small shifts in benthic cover including an increase in algae and decrease in sponges on Sonnier Bank (Rooker et al., in preparation). They also report some shifts in fish community composition and extralimital occurrences of the hard coral *Acropora* that is typically found in tropical reef systems. Shifts of fish community structure were likely caused by Hurricane Rita in September 2005, and the identification of extralimital corals in the Flower Garden Banks has been suggested as evidence for warmer waters in the general area (Zimmer, et al., 2006).

The MMS has conducted studies of select topographic features since Hurricane Rita passed directly over the Flower Garden Banks. Long-term monitoring has continued on a yearly basis at the East and West Flower Garden Banks through an equal partnership between MMS and NOAA's National Marine Sanctuary program. This monitoring not only expands MMS's knowledge and understanding of the Flower Garden Banks ecosystem, but it also improves the foundation from which management decisions are made. Another MMS study, *Post-Hurricane Assessment of Sensitive Habitats of the Flower Garden Banks Vicinity* (Precht et al., in preparation (a)), is investigating hurricane effects at the East Flower Garden, Sonnier, McGrail, Geyer, and Bright Banks. Initial assessment of the East Flower Garden Bank reveals mechanical damage from Hurricane Rita and a significant bleaching event (up to 46% of corals). This was followed by an outbreak of coral disease affecting up to 8 percent of corals at the East Flower Garden Bank. These are the most severe recorded outbreaks of bleaching and disease at the Flower Garden Banks. Other preliminary results suggest little hurricane damage to McGrail, Geyer, and Bright Banks but severe damage at Sonnier Bank (Precht et al., in preparation (a)). Speculation is that Sonnier Bank was more affected because of its shallower depth and position on the east side of the storm track. It is also thought that repeated anchor damage has affected Sonnier Bank. Community recovery is expected to take at least 5 years if further anchor damage is prevented. Monitoring at the Flower Garden Banks in 2006 and 2007 showed good recovery of corals with no significant deterioration of community health (Precht et al., 2006; Precht et al., in preparation (b)).

The MMS has reexamined the analysis for topographic features presented in the Multisale EIS, based on the additional information presented above. This new information documents the potential, somewhat severe impact caused by natural events, especially the cumulative impacts of hurricanes. However, OCS-related oil and gas impacts remain unchanged and previous assessments are still accurate. No new significant information was discovered that would alter the impact conclusion for topographic features presented in the Multisale EIS; therefore, a new analysis of the potential impacts of proposed Lease Sale 207 on topographic features is not required. The analysis and potential impacts detailed in the Multisale EIS still apply for proposed Lease Sale 207.

4.2.4.2. Continental Slope and Deepwater Resources

4.2.4.2.1. Chemosynthetic Deepwater Benthic Communities

The description of the biology, life history, and distribution of chemosynthetic deepwater benthic communities can be found in Chapter 3.2.2.2.1 of the Multisale EIS. A detailed impact analysis of the routine, accidental, and cumulative impacts of proposed Lease Sale 207 on chemosynthetic communities can be found in Chapters 4.2.1.4.2.1, 4.4.4.2.1, and 4.5.4.2 of the Multisale EIS, respectively. The following information is a summary of the impact analysis incorporated from the Multisale EIS. The location of known chemosynthetic communities in the northern Gulf of Mexico is shown in **Figure 7**.

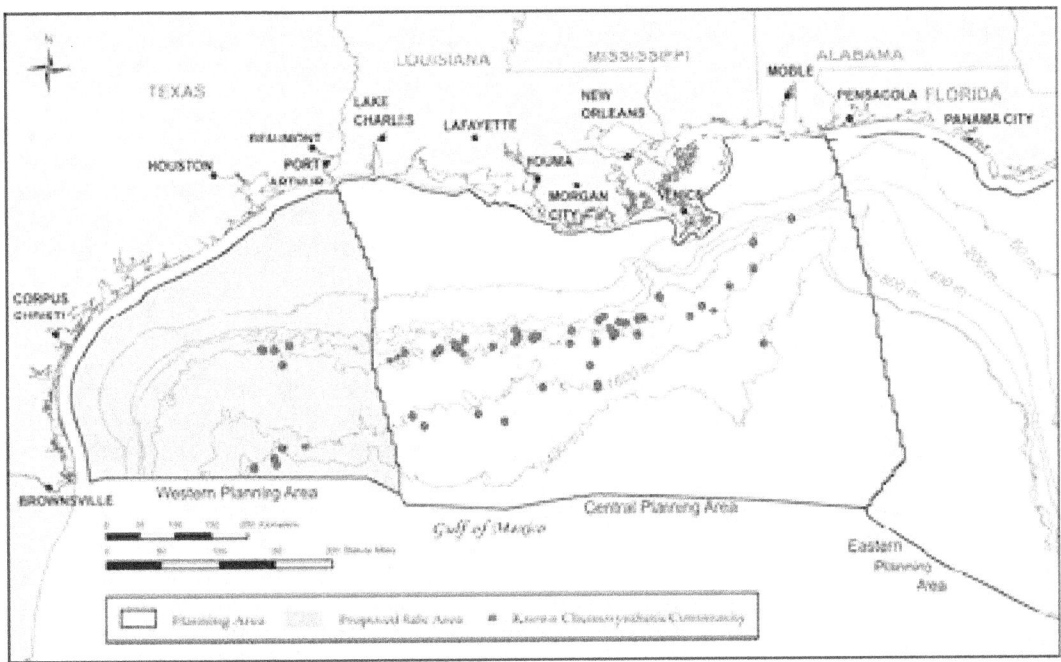

Figure 7.   Known Chemosynthetic Communities in the Northern Gulf of Mexico.

Chemosynthetic communities are susceptible to physical impacts from structure placement (including templates or subsea completions), anchoring, pipeline installation, or from a blowout depending on bottom-current conditions.   The guidance provided in NTL 2000-G20 greatly reduces the risk of these physical impacts by establishing standardized avoidance procedures for potential chemosynthetic communities identified during the plan and permit approval processes by such methods as geophysical survey records or photodocumentation.

If the presence of a high-density community was missed using existing procedures, potentially severe or catastrophic impacts could occur due to raking of the sea bottom by anchors and anchor chains from floating structures and partial or complete burial by mud and cuttings associated with pre-riser discharges or some types of riserless drilling.   Variations in the dispersal and toxicity of synthetic-based drilling fluids may contribute to the potential areal extent of these impacts.   The severity of such an impact is such that there would be incremental losses of productivity, reproduction, community relationships, and overall ecological functions of the community, and incremental damage to ecological relationships with the surrounding benthos.   Impacts on chemosynthetic communities from any accidental release of oil would be a remote possibility.

Impacts on deepwater communities in the Gulf of Mexico from sources other than OCS activities are considered negligible.   The incremental contribution of proposed Lease Sale 207 to the cumulative impact is expected to be slight, and to result from the effects of the possible impacts caused by physical disturbance of the seafloor and minor impacts from sediment resuspension.

Proposed Lease Sale 207 is expected to cause little damage to the ecological function or biological productivity of the widespread, low-density chemosynthetic communities.   NTL 2000-G20 expects an avoidance distance of a minimum 1,500 ft (457 m) for the rarer, widely scattered, high-density, Bush Hill-type chemosynthetic communities.   This avoidance distance reduces most impacts from drilling discharges and resuspended sediments.

A search was conducted for new information published since completion of the Multisale EIS.   A search of Internet information sources (including scientific journals) as well as interviews with personnel from academic institutions and governmental resource agencies was conducted to determine the availability of new information.   In addition, there is an ongoing MMS/National Oceanic and Atmospheric Administration Office of Ocean Exploration (NOAA-OE) co-sponsored research project, *Investigations of Chemosynthetic Communities on the Lower Continental Slope of the Gulf of Mexico,* specifically targeting chemosynthetic communities in the deep GOM (USDOI, MMS, 2006). This study was referenced in the Multisale EIS and is being tracked. Some new chemosynthetic communities were discovered in 2006 and 2007; however, they were located with the surveys required by the biological review process for plans or pipeline applications to determine the proximity of areas with potential chemosynthetic communities.

The MMS has reexamined the analysis for chemosynthetic communities presented in the Multisale EIS, based on the additional information presented above. No new significant information was discovered that would alter the impact conclusion for chemosynthetic communities presented in the Multisale EIS; therefore, a new analysis of the potential impacts of proposed Lease Sale 207 on chemosynthetic communities is not required. The analysis and potential impacts detailed in the Multisale EIS still apply for proposed Lease Sale 207.

4.2.4.2.2. *Nonchemosynthetic Deepwater Benthic Communities*

The description of the biology, life history, and distribution of nonchemosynthetic deepwater benthic communities can be found in Chapter 3.2.2.2.2 of the Multisale EIS. A detailed impact analysis of the routine, accidental, and cumulative impacts of proposed Lease Sale 207 on nonchemosynthetic communities can be found in Chapters 4.2.1.4.2.2, 4.4.4.2.2, and 4.5.4.2 of the Multisale EIS, respectively. The following information is a summary of the impact analysis incorporated from the Multisale EIS.

Some impact on soft-bottom, benthic communities from drilling and production activities would occur as a result of physical contact (crushing, burial) resulting from structure placement (including templates or subsea completions), anchoring, and installation of pipelines regardless of their locations. Megafauna and infauna communities at or below the sediment/water interface would be impacted from the muds and cuttings normally discharged at the seafloor at the start of every new well prior to riser installation. The impact from muds and cuttings discharged at the surface is expected to be low in deep water. Drilling muds would not be expected to reach the bottom in significant accumulations beyond a few hundred meters from the surface-discharge location, and cuttings would be dispersed. Even in situations where substantial burial of typical benthic infaunal communities occurred, recolonization from populations from neighboring soft-bottom substrate would be expected over a relatively short period of time for all size ranges of organisms, in a matter of days for bacteria, and probably less than 1 year for most all macrofauna species. Most benthic invertebrates have some adaptive strategy to avoid burial by sudden pulses of sediment having thicknesses less than approximately 1 ft (0.3 m) (USDOI, MMS, 2005; page 68).

Deepwater coral habitats and other potential hard-bottom communities not associated with chemosynthetic communities appear to be relatively rare. These unique communities are distinctive and similar in nature to protected topographic features on the continental shelf. Any hard substrate communities located in deep water would be particularly sensitive to impacts from OCS activities. Impacts on these sensitive habitats could permanently prevent recolonization with similar organisms requiring hard substrate.

Accidental events resulting from proposed Lease Sale 207 are expected to cause little damage to the ecological function or biological productivity of the widespread, typical, deep-sea benthic communities. Some impact on benthic communities would occur as a result of an accidental blowout. Megafauna and infauna communities at or below the sediment/water interface would be impacted by the physical disturbance of a blowout or by burial from resuspended sediments. Even in situations where substantial burial of typical benthic communities occurred due to a blowout, recolonization from populations from neighboring substrate would be expected over a relatively short period of time for all size ranges of organisms in the same timeframes as described above.

Impacts on deepwater communities in the Gulf of Mexico from sources other than OCS activities are considered negligible. The incremental contribution of proposed Lease Sale 207 to the cumulative impact is expected to be slight, and to result from the effects of the possible impacts caused by physical disturbance of the seafloor and minor impacts from sediment resuspension.

Proposed Lease Sale 207 is expected to cause little damage to the ecological function or biological productivity of the widespread, typical soft-bottom, deep-sea benthic communities. Impacts on other hard-bottom communities are expected to be avoided as a consequence of the application of the existing NTL 2000-G20 for chemosynthetic communities. The same geochemical conditions associated with the potential presence of chemosynthetic communities also results in the establishment of hard carbonate substrate that is generally avoided by burrowing infauna.

A search was conducted for new information published since completion of the Multisale EIS. A search of Internet information sources (including scientific journals) as well as interviews with personnel from academic institutions and governmental resource agencies was conducted to determine availability of new information.

Interest in deepwater corals has increased rapidly in the last decade as more coral systems are discovered worldwide and their importance in providing habitat for diverse communities is realized. The MMS recently published two studies on hard-bottom communities with an emphasis on the coral *Lophelia*. The following are summaries of the results of these two studies, which will be used to develop additional studies of hard-bottom habitats in the deep Gulf of Mexico and which will also enhance the ability of MMS to protect sensitive, deepwater biological features.

The report, *Characterization of Northern Gulf of Mexico Deepwater Hard-Bottom Communities with Emphasis on Lophelia Coral* (CSA, 2007), presents the results of a study of 10 sites on the northern Gulf of Mexico continental slope consisting of hard-bottom areas that generally include dense assemblages of the coral *Lophelia pertusa*. Study elements include geological characterization; biological characterization, imaging, and sampling; water chemistry; and physical oceanography including short-term and long-term current meter deployments. This was the first comprehensive study of the distribution of *Lophelia pertusa* and its biology and ecology in the Gulf of Mexico. Results suggest that *Lophelia pertusa* plays a significant role in the ecology of deepwater, hard-bottom habitats on the upper slope.

In addition, there is an ongoing MMS/NOAA-OE co-sponsored research project, *Investigations of Chemosynthetic Communities on the Lower Continental Slope of the Gulf of Mexico*, which also looked at other hard bottoms including nonchemosynthetic communities (USDOI, MMS, 2006). This study was referenced in the Multisale EIS and is being tracked. Some new deepwater coral communities were discovered in 2006 and 2007; however, they were located with the surveys required by the biological review process for plans or pipeline applications to determine the proximity of areas with potential chemosynthetic communities that also incorporates hard bottom and potential deepwater coral habitats.

The MMS has reexamined the analysis for nonchemosynthetic deepwater benthic communities presented in the Multisale EIS, based on the additional information presented above. No new significant information was discovered that would alter the impact conclusion for nonchemosynthetic deepwater benthic communities presented in the Multisale EIS; therefore, a new analysis of the potential impacts of proposed Lease Sale 207 on nonchemosynthetic, deepwater benthic communities is not required. The analysis and potential impacts detailed in the Multisale EIS still apply for proposed Lease Sale 207.

4.2.5. Marine Mammals

The description of the biology, life history, and distribution of marine mammals in the Gulf of Mexico can be found in Chapter 3.2.3 of the Multisale EIS. A detailed impact analysis of the routine, accidental and cumulative impacts of proposed Lease Sale 207 on marine mammals can be found in Chapters 4.2.1.5, 4.4.5, and 4.5.5 of the Multisale EIS, respectively. The following information is a summary of the impact analysis incorporated from the Multisale EIS.

Potential effects on marine mammal species may occur from routine activities associated with proposed Lease Sale 207 and may be direct or indirect. The major impact-producing factors affecting marine mammals as a result of routine OCS activities include the degradation of water quality from operational discharges; noise generated by helicopters, vessels, operating platforms, and drillships; vessel traffic; explosive structure removals; seismic surveys; and marine debris from service vessels and OCS structures.

Small numbers of marine mammals could be killed or injured by a collision with a service vessel; however, current MMS requirements and guidelines for vessel operation in the vicinity of protected species should minimize this risk (the proposed Protected Species Lease Stipulation and NTL 2007-G04).

Marine mammal ingestion of industry-generated debris, which is accidentally lost, is a concern. Sperm whales may be particularly at risk because of their suspected feeding behavior involving cruising along the bottom with their mouth open. Entanglement in debris could have serious consequences. A sperm whale could suffer diminished feeding and reproductive success, and potential injury, infection, and death from entanglement in lost packing materials or debris. Industry has made good progress in debris management on vessels and offshore structures in the last several years. The debris awareness training, instruction, and placards required by the proposed Protected Species Lease Stipulation and NTL 2007-G03 are intended to greatly minimize the amount of debris that is accidentally lost overboard by offshore personnel.

There is no conclusive evidence that anthropogenic noise has or has not caused long-term displacements of, or reductions in, marine mammal populations. Noise associated with proposed Lease Sale 207, including drilling noise, aircraft, and vessels, may affect marine mammals by eliciting a startle response or by masking other underwater sounds necessary for proper feeding or reproductive success. However, many of the industry-related sounds are believed to be out of, or on the limits of, marine mammal hearing, and the sounds are also generally temporary. The continued presence of sperm whales in close proximity to some of the deepwater structures in the GOM tends to lessen the concern of permanent displacement by disturbances caused by activity in support of offshore drilling or production.

Seismic operations have the potential to harm marine mammals in close proximity to firing airgun arrays, especially if they are directly beneath airguns when surveying begins. The proposed Protected Species Lease Stipulation and several mitigation measures, including onboard observers and airgun shut-downs for whales in the exclusion zone, included in NTL 2007-G02, "Implementation of Seismic Survey Mitigation Measures and Protected Species Observer Program," minimize the potential of harm from seismic operations to marine mammals.

Marine mammal death or injury is not expected from explosive structure-removal operations. Existing mitigations and those recently developed for structures placed in oceanic waters should continue to minimize adverse effects to marine mammals from these activities.

Contaminants in waste discharges and drilling muds might indirectly affect marine mammals through food-chain biomagnification. Although the scope and magnitude of such effects are not known, direct or indirect effects are not expected to be lethal.

Routine activities related to Lease Sale 207, particularly when mitigated as required by MMS, are not expected to have long-term adverse effects on the size and productivity of any marine mammal species or population endemic to the northern GOM.

Accidental blowouts, oil spills, and spill-response activities potentially resulting from Lease Sale 207 could impact marine mammals in the GOM. Characteristics of impacts (i.e., acute vs. chronic impacts) depend on the magnitude, frequency, location, and date of accidents; characteristics of spilled oil; spill-response capabilities and timing; and various meteorological and hydrological factors. Populations of marine mammals in the northern Gulf will be exposed to residual oils spilled as a result of Lease Sale 207 during their lifetimes; however, chronic or acute exposure is not expected to harass, harm, or have lethal or sublethal effects on marine mammals in the northern Gulf. Marine mammals made no apparent attempt to avoid spilled oil in some cases (Smultea and Würsig, 1995); however, marine mammals have been observed apparently detecting and avoiding slicks in other reports (Geraci and St. Aubin, 1987). Exposure to hydrocarbons persisting in the sea following the dispersal of a large oil slick is likely to result in sublethal impacts (e.g., decreased health, reproductive fitness, and longevity; and increased vulnerability to disease) to marine mammals.

Activities considered under the cumulative scenario could affect protected cetaceans and sirenians (manatees). Manatees, known to have occurred in the warm waters of Lake Pontchartrain in the weeks before Hurricane Katrina (Louisiana Dept. of Wildlife and Fisheries, 2005), are generally extralimital in western Louisiana and Texas and are rare in waters of the WPA. Protected cetaceans could be impacted by the degradation of water quality resulting from operational discharges, vessel traffic, noise generated by platforms, drillships, helicopters and vessels, seismic surveys, explosive structure removals, oil spills, oil-spill-response activities, loss of debris from service vessels and OCS structures, commercial fishing, capture and removal, and pathogens.

The cumulative impact on marine mammals is expected to result in a number of chronic and sporadic sublethal effects (behavioral effects and nonfatal exposure to or intake of OCS-related contaminants or debris) that may stress and/or weaken individuals of a local group or population and predispose them to infection from natural or anthropogenic sources. Few deaths are expected from oil spills, chance collisions with OCS service vessels, ingestion of plastic material, commercial fishing, and pathogens. Oil spills of any size are estimated to be recurring events that would periodically contact marine mammals. Deaths as a result of structure removals are not expected to occur due to mitigation measures (e.g., NMFS Observer Program). Disturbance (noise from vessel traffic and drilling operations, etc.) and/or exposure to sublethal levels of toxins and anthropogenic contaminants may stress animals, weaken their immune systems, and make them more vulnerable to parasites and diseases that normally would not be fatal. The net result of any disturbance would be dependent upon the size and percentage of the population likely to be affected, the ecological importance of the disturbed area, the environmental and biological parameters that influence an animal's sensitivity to disturbance and stress, or the accommodation time in response to prolonged disturbance (Geraci and St. Aubin, 1980). Collisions between cetaceans and ships, although expected to be rare events, could cause serious injury or mortality. Natural phenomenon, such as tropical storms and hurricanes, are impossible to predict, but they are expected in the GOM. Generally, the offshore species and the offshore habitat are not expected to have been severely affected in the long term. Species that occupy more nearshore habitats, however, may have suffered more long-term impacts.

Effects of the incremental contribution of proposed Lease Sale 207, combined with non-OCS activities, may be deleterious to cetaceans occurring in the GOM. Biological significance of any mortality would depend, in part, on the size and reproductive rates of the affected stocks, as well as the number, age, and size of animals affected.

The ESA (16 U.S.C. 1631 *et seq.*), as amended (43 U.S.C. 1331 *et seq.*), establishes a national policy designed to protect and conserve threatened and endangered species and the ecosystems upon which they depend. The ESA is administered by FWS and NMFS. Section 7 of the ESA governs interagency cooperation and consultation. Under Section 7, MMS consults with FWS and NMFS to ensure that OCS activities under MMS jurisdiction do not jeopardize the continued existence of threatened or endangered species and/or result in adverse modification or destruction of their critical habitat.

The formal consultation with NMFS was concluded with receipt of the Biological Opinion (BO) on July 3, 2007 (USDOC, NMFS, 2007a). The BO concludes that the proposed lease sales and associated activities in the GOM in the 2007-2012 OCS Leasing Program, which includes Lease Sale 207, are not likely to jeopardize the continued existence of threatened and endangered species under NMFS jurisdiction or destroy or adversely modify designated critical habitat.

Section 7(b)(4)(c) of the ESA specifies that, in order to provide an incidental take statement for an endangered or threatened species of marine mammal, the taking must be authorized under Section 101(a)(5) of the Marine Mammal Protection Act (MMPA). Since no incidental take of listed marine mammals is expected or has been authorized under Section 101(a)(5)(A) of the MMPA and/or its 1994 amendments (see ESA Section 7(b)(4)(C)), no statement on incidental take of endangered whales is provided and no take is authorized. Nevertheless, MMS must immediately notify (within 24 hours, if communication is possible) the NMFS' Office of Protected Resources should a take of a listed marine mammal occur.

On December 26, 2002, MMS submitted a request for 5-year regulations under the MMPA for the taking, by harassment, of sperm whales incidental to the oil and gas industry's seismic surveys to discover oil and gas deposits offshore in the GOM. The NMFS published an Advance Notice of Proposed Rulemaking regarding the small take authorization on March 3, 2003 (68 FR 9991). Following issuance of such regulations under the MMPA, NMFS will amend this opinion to include any authorized incidental take of sperm whales, as may be appropriate at that time.

The NMFS believes that a small number of listed species will experience adverse effects as the result of exposure to a large oil spill or ingestion of accidentally spilled oil over the lifetime of the action. Spilled oil resulting from proposed Lease Sale 207 could take up to 11 nonlethal takes of sperm whales over the 40-year lifetime of the proposed lease sale. However, NMFS is not including an incidental take statement for the incidental take of listed species due to oil exposure. Incidental take, as defined at 50 CFR 402.02, refers only to takings that result from an otherwise lawful activity. The Clean Water Act (33 U.S.C. 1251 *et seq.*) as amended by the Oil Pollution Act of 1990 (33 U.S.C. 2701 *et seq.*) prohibits discharges of harmful quantities of oil, as defined at 40 CFR 110.3, into waters of the United States. Therefore, even though the BO considered the effects on listed species by oil spills that may result from proposed Lease Sale 207, those takings that would result from an unlawful activity (i.e., oil spills) are not specified in this Incidental Take Statement and have no protective coverage under Section 7(o)(2) of the ESA.

The following information was present in the BO, but not in the Multisale EIS. Based on NOAA surveys, opportunistic sightings, whaling catches, and stranding records, sperm whales in the GOM occur year-round. Sperm whales appear to favor water depths of about 1,000 m (3,281 ft) and appear to be concentrated in at least two geographic regions of the northern GOM: an area off the Dry Tortugas and offshore of the Mississippi River delta (Maze-Foley and Mullin, 2006); however, distribution also appears influenced by occurrence and movement of cyclonic/anticyclonic currents in the GOM.

The FWS and MMS have consulted informally per FWS guidance on proposed Lease Sale 207. As a result, there were no new mitigations or Terms and Conditions from FWS.

A recent report presents the results of a study that collected dive patterns of sperm whales in the Atlantic Ocean to compare with the dive patterns and social structure of sperm whales in the Gulf of Mexico (Palka and Johnson, 2007). The study started a baseline of line transect, photo-identification, oceanographic, and genetic data for the Atlantic sperm whale. Compared with the Delta region in the Gulf of Mexico, parts of the Atlantic Ocean may serve as a control population of sperm whales with little exposure to sounds of oil- and gas-related activities. The study found Gulf of Mexico sperm whales follow a foraging and socializing cycle similar to that seen for the North Atlantic whales, but North Atlantic sperm whales dive significantly deeper (average 934 m (3,064 ft) compared with 639 m (2,096 ft) for GOM whales) when foraging (Palka and Johnson, 2007).

The MMS has reexamined the analysis for marine mammals presented in the Multisale EIS, based on the additional information presented above. No new significant information was discovered that would alter the impact conclusion for marine mammals presented in the Multisale EIS; therefore, a new analysis of the potential impacts of proposed Lease Sale 207 on marine mammals is not required. The analysis and potential impacts detailed in the Multisale EIS still apply for proposed Lease Sale 207.

4.2.6. Sea Turtles

The description of the biology, life history, and distribution of sea turtles in the Gulf of Mexico can be found in Chapter 3.2.4 of the Multisale EIS. A detailed impact analysis of the routine, accidental, and cumulative impacts of proposed Lease Sale 207 on sea turtles can be found in Chapters 4.2.1.6, 4.4.6, and 4.5.6 of the Multisale EIS, respectively. The following information is a summary of the impact analysis incorporated from the Multisale EIS.

Routine activities resulting from proposed Lease Sale 207 have the potential to harm sea turtles. These animals could be impacted by the degradation of water quality resulting from operational discharges; noise generated by seismic exploration, helicopter and vessel traffic, platforms and platform lighting, and drillships; vessel collisions; and marine debris generated by service vessels and OCS facilities. Lethal effects are most likely to be from chance collisions with OCS service vessels and ingestion of plastic materials. Most OCS activities are expected to have sublethal effects.

Contaminants in waste discharges and drilling muds might indirectly affect sea turtles through food-chain biomagnification, but there is uncertainty concerning the possible effects. Rapid dilution of the discharges should minimize impact. Chronic sublethal effects (e.g., stress) resulting in persistent physiological or behavioral changes and/or avoidance of impacted areas from noise disturbance could cause declines in survival or fecundity and result in population declines; however, such declines are not expected. The required seismic operation mitigations, particularly clearance of the impact area of sea turtles prior to ramp-up, and the subsequent gradual ramping up of the airguns, should minimize the impact of rapid onset of, and close proximity to, very loud noise. Vessel traffic is a serious threat to sea turtles. Diligence on the part of vessel operators, as encouraged by the vessel strike mitigations, should minimize vessel/sea turtle collisions. Actual sea turtle impacts from explosive removals in recent years have been small. The updated pre- and post-detonation mitigations should ensure that injuries remain extremely rare. Brightly lit offshore platforms can attract and disorient turtle hatchlings. Greatly improved handling of waste and trash by industry, along with the annual awareness training required by the marine debris mitigations, is decreasing the occurrence of plastics in the ocean and minimizing the devastating effects on sea turtles that may ingest plastic, mistaking it for food. The routine activities of proposed Lease Sale 207 are unlikely to have significant adverse effects on the size and recovery of any sea turtle species or population in the GOM.

Accidental blowouts, oil spills, and spill-response activities resulting from proposed Lease Sale 207 have the potential to impact small to large numbers of sea turtles in the GOM, depending on the magnitude and frequency of accidents, the ability to respond to accidents, the location and date of accidents, and various meteorological and hydrological factors. Populations of sea turtles in the northern Gulf could be exposed to residuals of oil accidentally spilled as a result of proposed Lease Sale 207 during their lifetimes. Chronic or acute exposure may result in the harassment, harm, or mortality of sea turtles occurring in the northern Gulf. In most foreseeable cases, exposure to hydrocarbons persisting in the sea following the dispersal of an oil slick will result in sublethal impacts (e.g., decreased health, reproductive fitness, and longevity; and increased vulnerability to disease) to sea turtles. Sea turtle hatchling exposure to, fouling by, or consumption of tarballs persisting in the sea following the dispersal of an oil slick would likely be fatal. Ingestion of floating plastics that could be mistaken for a favorite food source—jellyfish—can bind the digestive system and weaken the animal, making it susceptible to starvation or infection.

Activities considered under the cumulative scenario may harm sea turtles and their habitats. Those activities include structure installation, dredging, water quality and habitat degradation, OCS-related marine debris, vessel traffic, seismic surveys, explosive structure removals, oil spills, oil-spill-response activities, natural catastrophes, pollution, dredge operations, vessel collisions, commercial and recreational fishing, human consumption, beach lighting, and power plant entrainment. Sea turtles could be killed or injured by chance collision with vessels or eating foreign materials mistaken for food. It is expected that deaths as a result of structure removals would rarely occur because of mitigation measures. The presence of, and noise produced by, service vessels and by the construction, operation, and removal of drill rigs may cause physiological stress and make animals more susceptible to disease or predation, as well as disrupt normal activities. Contaminants in waste discharges and drilling muds might indirectly affect sea turtles through food-chain biomagnification.

Oil spills and oil-spill-response activities are potential threats that may be expected to cause turtle deaths. Contact with, and consumption of oil and oil-contaminated prey, may seriously impact turtles. Sea turtles have been seriously harmed by oil spills in the past. The majority of OCS activities are estimated to be sublethal (behavioral effects and nonfatal exposure to intake of OCS-related contaminants or debris). Chronic sublethal effects (e.g., stress) resulting in persistent physiological or behavioral changes and/or avoidance of impacted areas could cause declines in survival or productivity, resulting in either acute or gradual population declines. However, mitigations currently in place have, and will continue to, minimize sea turtle impacts. Natural phenomenon, such as tropical storms and hurricanes, are impossible to predict, but they are expected in the GOM. Generally, the offshore species and the offshore habitat are not expected to be severely affected in the long-term. However, species that occupy habitats nearer to shore and those that use nearshore habitats in the WPA for nesting may suffer more long-term impacts. The incremental contribution of proposed Lease Sale 207 to the numerous, cumulative impacts on sea turtles is not expected to be significant, especially due to mitigations currently in place.

The ESA (16 U.S.C. 1631 *et seq.*), as amended (43 U.S.C. 1331 *et seq.*), establishes a national policy designed to protect and conserve threatened and endangered species and the ecosystems upon which they depend. The ESA is administered by FWS and NMFS. Section 7 of the ESA governs interagency cooperation and consultation. Under Section 7, MMS consults with FWS and NMFS to ensure that OCS activities under MMS jurisdiction do not jeopardize the continued existence of threatened or endangered species and/or result in adverse modification or destruction of their critical habitat.

The formal consultation with NMFS was concluded with receipt of the BO on July 3, 2007 (USDOC, NMFS, 2007a). The BO concludes that the proposed lease sales and associated activities in the GOM in the 2007-2012 OCS Leasing Program, which includes Lease Sale 207, are not likely to jeopardize the continued existence of threatened and endangered species under NMFS jurisdiction, or destroy or adversely modify designated critical habitat. The NMFS issued an Incidental Take Statement on sea turtle species; the Statement contains reasonable and prudent measures (RPM's) with implementing terms and conditions to help minimize take.

The NMFS has determined that the following RPM's are necessary and appropriate to minimize impacts of the incidental take of sea turtles from vessel operation.

(1) The MMS must reduce the potential for sea turtles to be struck and injured by vessels operating in support of oil and gas development activities in the GOM.

(2) The MMS must require the monitoring and reporting of any sea turtles struck or observed to have sign of vessel interaction to assess the actual level of incidental take in comparison with the anticipated incidental take.

In order to be exempt from liability for take prohibited by Section 9 of the ESA, MMS must comply with the following terms and conditions, which implement the RPM's described above. These terms and conditions are nondiscretionary.

The following terms and conditions implement RPM No. 1.

(1) The MMS must implement NMFS measures to reduce the risk of accidental vessel strikes with sea turtles by use of its legal authorities to ensure implementation of, and compliance with NTL No 2007-G04.

The following terms and conditions implement RPM No. 2.

(1) The MMS must make information available to vessel operators concerning species information on sea turtles in the GOM and reporting of vessel-struck, or injured and dead animals.

(2) The MMS must ensure that all vessel-struck, or injured or dead turtles with indications of vessel interactions are reported to the Sea Turtle Stranding Network Coordinator in the nearest coastal state. Any takes of listed species shall be reported to the NMFS Southeast Regional Office within no more than 24 hours of the incident to takereport.nmfssen@noaa.gov. If an MMS action is responsible for the injured or dead animals (e.g., because of a vessel strike), MMS shall require the responsible parties to assist the respective salvage and stranding network as appropriate. Report dead or injured protected species to your local stranding network contacts.

(3) The MMS must submit an annual report to NMFS Southeast Regional Office regarding the reports of vessel-struck sea turtles, and injured or dead sea turtles reported from oil and gas operators. Hardcopies of all annual reports will be submitted to the following address:

> Assistant Regional Administrator for Protected Resources
> National Marine Fisheries Service
> 263 13th Avenue South
> St. Petersburg, FL 33701

The NMFS expects impacts on sea turtles in the proposed lease sale area as a result of OCS oil and gas leasing activities. Based on stranding records, incidental captures during recreational and commercial fishing operations, scientific surveys, and historical data, the five species of sea turtles are known to occur in GOM waters in and around the proposed lease sale area. The vessel strike avoidance requirements (NTL 2003-G10) will appreciably reduce the numbers of sea turtles that may be incidentally taken from routine offshore vessel operations associated with proposed Lease Sale 207; however, the available information on the relationship between these species and OCS oil and gas activities indicates that sea turtles may be killed or injured by vessel strikes as a result of proposed Lease Sale 207. Therefore, pursuant to Section 7(b)(4) of the ESA, NMFS anticipates incidental take as follows:

- 119 lethal takes (2.9 individuals annually, on average) and 238 nonlethal takes (5.9 individuals annually, on average) of loggerhead sea turtles over the 40-year lifetime of proposed Lease Sale 207.

- 10 lethal takes (1 individual every 4 years, on average) and 21 nonlethal takes (1 individual every 1.9 years, on average) of leatherback sea turtles over the 40-year lifetime of proposed Lease Sale 207.

- 13 lethal takes (1 individual every 3 years, on average) and 26 nonlethal takes (1 individual every 1.5 years, on average) of Kemp's ridley sea turtles over the 40-year lifetime of proposed Lease Sale 207.

- 38 lethal takes (1 individual every 1.1 years, on average) and 76 nonlethal takes (1.9 individuals annually, on average) of green sea turtles over the 40-year lifetime of proposed Lease Sale 207.

- 1 lethal take and 1 nonlethal take of a hawksbill sea turtle over the 40-year lifetime of proposed Lease Sale 207.

If the actual incidental take exceeds this level, MMS must immediately reinitiate formal consultation. The NMFS believes that a small number of listed species will experience adverse effects as the result of exposure to a large oil spill or ingestion of accidentally spilled oil over the lifetime of proposed Lease Sale 207. Spilled oil resulting from proposed Lease Sale 207 could take up to 42 lethal and 111 nonlethal takes of loggerheads; 2 lethal and 7 nonlethal takes of a leatherback sea turtles; 9 lethal and 16 nonlethal takes of Kemp's ridley sea turtles; and 13 lethal and 36 nonlethal take of green sea turtles over the 40-year lifetime of the proposed lease sale. However, NMFS is not including an Incidental Take Statement for the incidental take of listed species due to oil exposure. Incidental take, as defined at 50 CFR 402.02, refers only to takings that result from an otherwise lawful activity. The Clean Water Act (33 U.S.C. 1251 *et seq.*), as amended by OPA (33 U.S.C. 2701 *et seq.*), prohibits discharges of harmful quantities of oil, as defined at 40 CFR 110.3, into waters of the United States. Therefore, even though the BO considered the effects on listed species by oil spills that may result from proposed Lease Sale 207, those takings that would result from an unlawful activity (i.e., oil spills) are not specified in the Incidental Take Statement and have no protective coverage under Section 7(o)(2) of the ESA.

The FWS and MMS have consulted informally per FWS guidance on Lease Sale 207. As a result, there were no new mitigations or Terms and Conditions from FWS. The MMS has reexamined the analysis for sea turtles presented in the Multisale EIS, based on the additional information presented above. No new significant information was discovered that would alter the impact conclusion for sea turtles presented in the Multisale EIS; therefore, a new analysis of the potential impacts of proposed Lease Sale 207 on sea turtles is not required. The analysis and potential impacts detailed in the Multisale EIS still apply for proposed Lease Sale 207.

4.2.7. Coastal and Marine Birds

The description of the biology, life history, and distribution of coastal and marine birds in the Gulf of Mexico can be found in Chapter 3.2.5 of the Multisale EIS. A detailed impact analysis of the routine, accidental, and cumulative impacts of proposed Lease Sale 207 on coastal and marine birds can be found in Chapters 4.2.1.1.7, 4.4.8, and 4.5.8 of the Multisale EIS, respectively. The following information is a summary of the impact analysis incorporated from the Multisale EIS.

The majority of effects resulting from proposed Lease Sale 207 on endangered/threatened and nonendangered/nonthreatened coastal and marine birds are expected to be sublethal: behavioral effects, sublethal exposure to or intake of OCS-related contaminants or debris, temporary disturbances, and displacement of localized groups from impacted habitats. Chronic sublethal stress, however, is often undetectable in birds. As a result of stress, individuals may weaken, facilitating infection and disease; then, migratory species may not have the strength to reach their destination. Attraction to platform lights may result in the circling of platforms, collision with and subsequent stranding on the platform/vessel, and wasted use of important energy reserves that causes acute sublethal stress from energy loss, while stopovers on platforms would reduce energy loss. No significant habitat impacts are expected to occur directly from routine activities resulting from proposed Lease Sale 207. Secondary impacts from pipeline and navigation canals to coastal habitats will occur over the long-term and may ultimately displace species from traditional sites to alternative sites.

Oil spills from proposed Lease Sale 207 pose the greatest potential direct and indirect impacts on coastal and marine birds. Birds that are heavily oiled are usually killed. If physical oiling of individuals or local groups of birds occurs, some degree of both acute and chronic physiological stress associated with direct and secondary uptake of oil would be expected. Small coastal spills, pipeline spills, and spills from accidents in navigated waterways can contact and affect the different groups of coastal and marine birds, most commonly marsh birds, waders, waterfowl, and certain shorebirds. Lightly oiled birds can sustain tissue and organ damage from oil ingested during feeding and grooming or from oil that is inhaled. Stress, trauma, and shock enhance the effects of exposure and poisoning. Low levels of oil could stress birds by interfering with food detection, feeding impulses, predator avoidance, territory definition, homing of migratory species, susceptibility to physiological disorders, disease resistance, growth rates, reproduction, and respiration. Reproductive success can be affected by the toxins in oil. Indirect effects occur by fouling of nesting habitat, and displacement of individuals, breeding pairs, or populations to less favorable habitats. Competition may displace refugee seabirds from all habitats.

New research, experience, and testing will help the efficacy of the rehabilitation of oiled birds and probably improve scare methods that will keep birds away from an oil slick. Rehabilitation can be significant to the survival of threatened and endangered bird species.

Dispersants used in spill cleanup activity can have toxic effects similar to oil on the reproductive success of coastal and marine birds. The air, vehicle, and foot traffic that takes place during shoreline cleanup activity can disturb nesting populations and degrade or destroy habitat if not properly regulated.

Activities considered under the cumulative activities scenario will detrimentally affect coastal and marine birds. It is expected that the majority of effects from the major impact-producing factors on coastal and marine birds are sublethal (behavioral effects and nonfatal exposure to or intake of OCS-related contaminants or debris) and will usually cause temporary disturbances and displacement of localized groups inshore. The net effect of habitat loss from oil spills, new construction, and maintenance and use of pipeline corridors and navigation waterways will alter species composition and reduce the overall carrying capacity of disturbed area(s) in general.

The incremental contributions of proposed Lease Sale 207 (Chapters 4.2.1.1.7 and 4.4.8 of the Multisale EIS) to the cumulative impacts on coastal and marine birds is negligible because the effects of the most probable impacts, such as sale-related operational discharges and helicopters and service-vessel noise and traffic, are estimated to be sublethal, and some displacement of local individuals or groups may occur. It is expected that there will be little interaction between oil spills from proposed Lease Sale 207 and coastal and marine birds.

The cumulative effect of programmatic activities on coastal and marine birds is expected to result in a small but discernible decline in the numbers of birds with associated change in species composition and distribution. Some of these changes are expected to be permanent, as exemplified in historic census data, and to stem from a net decrease in preferred and/or critical habitat.

A search was conducted for new information published since completion of the Multisale EIS. A search of Internet bibliographic databases, Google (2007), and OCLC FirstSearch (2007), as well as personal interviews with authors of references used in the Multisale EIS was conducted to determine the availability of recent information since publication of the Multisale EIS. No new information was discovered from these information sources.

On June 28, 2007, FWS announced the removal of the bald eagle from the list of threatened and endangered species (USDOI, FWS, 2007a). The FWS will work with State wildlife agencies to monitor eagles for at least 5 years. The FWS can propose to relist the species if it appears that bald eagles again need the protection of the Endangered Species Act. The bald eagle will continue to be protected by the Bald and Golden Eagle Protection Act and the Migratory Bird Treaty Act. Both Federal laws prohibit "taking"—killing, selling, or otherwise harming eagles, their nests, or eggs.

Authors were contacted and interviewed to investigate any recent published data that may be available. A large study of military aircraft and the impacts of noise on birds offshore of California is in preparation, but it is not expected out soon (Bowles, personal communication, 2007). Nisbet (personal communication, 2007) knows of no new information on the impacts of human disturbance on birds since his own work in 2000. Flint (personal communication, 2007) knows of no new published information in 2006-2007 on the impacts of trash and debris on marine birds, particularly those with which she was familiar in the Pacific, including albatrosses at Midway Island. Jankowski (personal communication, 2007) suggested several articles from online bibliographic databases.

A literature search found Burger (1997), who reports that exposure to small amounts of oil may weaken birds or decrease their body weight so they live for years without problems until they face a severe environmental stress that can cause higher mortality rates than in unexposed birds. Burger (1993) notes little or no correlation between spill volume and bird mortality; rather, the density of seabirds in the affected area, wind conditions, wave action, and distance to the shore may have more effect. Khan and Ryan (1991) note substantial mortality in seabirds after attempts at rehabilitation. Sublethal symptoms of contamination were numerous and substantial prior to the mortality. Similarly, numerous symptoms were found in dead birds on the shore and in birds dying after rehabilitation that were affected by the *Prestige* oil spill in Spain on November 19, 2002 (Balseiro et al., 2005). Final major impacts on European shags (*Phalacrocorax aristotelis*) from the *Prestige* spill probably came in 2003 from a decimated food supply of fish (Velando et al., 2005). As oil weathered, the exposure of seabirds to oil from the *Exxon Valdez* spill shifted from direct oiling to ingestion with food (Hartung, 1995).

Parsons (1994) provides the following unique before and after data for impacts of a spill on birds. Extensive shoreline and salt marsh were oiled by a January 1990 Exxon spill in the Arthur Kill and Kill van Kull estuaries of New York Harbor. Double-crested cormorants had reached their pre-spill population growth by 1991. Productivity of herring gulls remained unchanged by the spill. Most heron populations increased after the spill. Great black-backed gulls had a loss of abundance. Snowy egrets and glossy ibis used salt marsh and mud flat habitat, some of which was oiled. Black-crowned night heron and glossy ibis had delayed nesting after the spill, and along with snowy egret showed lower reproductive success after the spill. Egg laying and hatching were generally more successful than chick-rearing, due to food shortages for chicks. Waterfowl were not affected seriously, except for a short-term decline in mallards.

The piping plover (*Charadrius melodus*), listed as threatened, is a migratory shorebird that is endemic to North America. It winters on the Atlantic and Gulf Coasts from North Carolina to Mexico and in the Bahamas West Indies. Critical wintering habitat includes the land between mean low water and any densely vegetated habitat, which is not already used by piping plover. It has been hypothesized that specific wintering habitat, which includes coastal sand flats and mud flats in close proximity to large inlets or passes, may attract the largest concentrations of piping plovers because of a preferred prey base and/or because the substrate coloration provides protection from aerial predators due to chromatic matching, or camouflage (Nicholls and Baldassarre, 1990). This species remains in a precarious state given its low population numbers, sparse distribution, and continued threats to habitat throughout its range. About 2,299 birds were located on the U.S. wintering grounds during the 2001 census (Haig and Ferland, 2002). Although the results of the 2006 International Census have not yet been published, during that census, 226 piping plovers were counted at 26 sites along 201.7 km in Louisiana (Smith, personal communication, 2007). At last count, the species' Atlantic population was down to fewer than 1,800 pairs (Barcott, 2007).

The MMS has reexamined the analysis for coastal and marine birds presented in the Multisale EIS, based on the additional information presented above. No new significant information was discovered that would alter the impact conclusion for coastal and marine birds presented in the Multisale EIS; therefore, a new analysis of the potential impacts of proposed Lease Sale 207 on coastal and marine birds is not required. The analysis and potential impacts detailed in the Multisale EIS still apply for proposed Lease Sale 207.

4.2.8. Fish Resources and Essential Fish Habitat

The description of the biology, life history, and distribution of fish resources and descriptions of essential fish habitat (EFH) can be found in Chapter 3.2.8.1 and 3.2.8.2 of the Multisale EIS, respectively. A detailed impact analysis of the routine, accidental, and cumulative impacts of proposed Lease Sale 207 on fish resources and EFH can be found in Chapters 4.2.1.1.8, 4.4.10, and 4.5.10 of the Multisale EIS, respectively. The following information is a summary of the impact analysis incorporated from the Multisale EIS.

It is expected that coastal and marine environmental degradation from proposed Lease Sale 207 would have little effect on fish resources or EFH. The impact of coastal and marine environmental degradation is expected to cause an undetectable decrease in fish resources or in EFH. Fish resources and EFH are expected to recover from more than 99 percent, but not all, of the expected coastal and marine environmental degradation. Fish populations, if left undisturbed, will regenerate in one generation, but any loss of wetlands as EFH would likely be permanent.

Routine activities such as pipeline trenching and OCS discharge of drilling muds and produced water would cause negligible impacts and would not deleteriously affect fish resources or EFH. At the expected level of impact, the resultant influence on fish resources would cause less than a 1 percent change in fish populations or EFH. As a result, there would be little disturbance to fish resources or EFH.

Accidental events resulting from oil and gas development in the proposed Lease Sale 207 area of the GOM have the potential to cause some detrimental effects on fisheries and commercial fishing practices. A subsurface blowout would have a negligible effect on GOM fish resources. If spills due to proposed

Lease Sale 207 were to occur in open waters of the OCS proximate to mobile adult finfish or shellfish, the effects would likely be nonfatal and the extent of damage would be reduced due to the capability of adult fish and shellfish to avoid a spill, to metabolize hydrocarbons, and to excrete both metabolites and parent compounds (recognizing that spill impacts are substantial when contacting fish eggs and larvae). The effect of proposed Lease Sale 207-related oil spills on fish resources is expected to cause less than a 1 percent decrease in standing stocks of any population, landings, or value of those landings. Historically, there have been no oil spills of any size that have had a long-term impact on fishery populations.

Additional hard substrate habitat provided by structure installation in areas where natural hard bottom is rare will tend to increase fish populations. Removal of these structures will eliminate that habitat except when decommissioning results in platforms being utilized as artificial reef material. This practice is expected to increase over time.

Activities resulting from other OCS Program and non-OCS events in the northern GOM have the potential to cause detrimental effects on fish resources and EFH. Impact-producing factors of the cumulative scenario that are expected to substantially affect fish resources and EFH include coastal and marine environmental degradation, overfishing, and to a lesser degree, coastal petroleum spills and coastal pipeline trenching. At the estimated level of cumulative impact, from OCS Program and non-OCS events, the resultant influence on fish resources and EFH is expected to be substantial, but not easily distinguished from effects due to natural population variations.

The incremental contribution of proposed Lease Sale 207's impacts on fish resources and EFH to the cumulative impact is small. The effects of impact-producing factors (coastal and marine environmental degradation, petroleum spills, subsurface blowouts, pipeline trenching, and offshore discharges of drilling muds and produced waters) related to proposed Lease Sale 207 are expected to be negligible (resulting in less than a 1% decrease in fish populations or EFH) and almost undetectable among the other cumulative impacts. Even with consideration of an extreme year of major hurricane impacts on coastal wetlands in 2005, the cumulative impact of proposed Lease Sale 207 is expected to be negligible and undetectable.

At the expected level of impact, the resultant influence on fish populations and EFH from proposed Lease Sale 207 would be negligible and indistinguishable from variations due to natural causes; however, wetland loss could occur due to a petroleum spill contacting inland areas. Proposed Lease Sale 207 is expected to result in less than a 1 percent decrease in fish resources and/or standing stocks or in EFH. It would require one generation for fish resources to recover from 99 percent of the impacts. Recovery from the loss of wetlands habitat would probably not occur.

A search was conducted for new information published since completion of the Multisale EIS. A search of Internet information sources (including scientific journals) as well as interviews with personnel from academic institutions and governmental resource agencies was conducted to determine availability of new information. Significant informational Internet websites include those from the Gulf of Mexico Fisheries Management Council and the NMFS Southeast Region. Some recent reports from NOAA have further documented impacts from the 2005 hurricanes on fish and fishery habitat. One very recent example is *Report to Congress on the Impact of Hurricanes Katrina, Rita, and Wilma on Commercial and Recreational Fishery Habitat of Alabama, Florida, Louisiana, Mississippi, and Texas*, which was published in July 2007 (USDOC, NMFS, 2007b). This report confirms the substantial impacts of the 2005 hurricanes to nearshore habitats, especially oyster reefs. Offshore fisheries habitat sustained some impact, but not substantial. Similar information was also presented in the Multisale EIS.

The status of fish stocks in the Gulf of Mexico has also been tracked. A recent report to Congress (USDOC, NMFS, 2007c) concluded, "With the exception of oysters, available information indicates Gulf Coast marine resources were not significantly impacted by the 2005 hurricanes." In the most recent quarter through June 2007, there were no major changes in the fish stock sustainability index (FSSI) reported by NMFS (USDOC, NMFS, 2007c). The following are the only changes in overfished status of FSSI stocks in the Southeast Region (April 1-June 30):

- *South Atlantic Gag* is now approaching an overfished condition.

- *Dolphin* is now above 80 percent of maximum sustainable yield.

- *Gulf of Mexico Red Grouper* is now rebuilt.

The MMS has reexamined the analysis for fish resources and EFH presented in the Multisale EIS, based on the additional information presented above. No new significant information was discovered that would alter the impact conclusion for fish resources and EFH presented in the Multisale EIS; therefore, a new analysis of the potential impacts of proposed Lease Sale 207 on fish resources and EFH is not required. The analysis and potential impacts detailed in the Multisale EIS still apply for proposed Lease Sale 207.

4.2.9. Commercial Fishing

The description of commercial fishing in the proposed Lease Sale 207 area can be found in Chapter 3.3.1 of the Multisale EIS. A detailed impact analysis of the routine, accidental, and cumulative impacts of proposed Lease Sale 207 on commercial fishing can be found in Chapters 4.2.1.1.9, 4.4.10, and 4.5.11 of the Multisale EIS, respectively. The following information is a summary of the impact analysis incorporated from the Multisale EIS.

Effects on commercial fishing from activities associated with proposed Lease Sale 207 could result from the installation of production platforms, underwater OCS obstructions, production platform removals, seismic surveys, subsurface blowouts, pipeline trenching, and petroleum spills. Activities such as seismic surveys and pipeline trenching will cause negligible impacts and will not deleteriously affect commercial fishing activities. Seismic surveys are not expected to cause long-term or permanent displacement of any listed species from critical habitat/preferred habitat or to result in the destruction or adverse modification of critical habitat or essential fish habitat. Operations such as production platform emplacement, underwater OCS impediments, and explosive platform removal will cause slightly greater impacts on commercial fishing.

Commercial fishermen would actively avoid the area of a spill. Even if fish resources successfully avoid spills, tainting (oily-tasting fish), public perception of tainting, or the potential of tainting commercial catches would prevent fishermen (either voluntarily or imposed by regulation) from initiating activities in the spill area. This, in turn, could decrease landings and/or the value of catch for several months. The effect of proposed Lease Sale 207-related oil spills on fish resources and commercial fishing is expected to cause less than a 1 percent decrease in standing stocks of any population, commercial fishing efforts, landings, or value of those landings.

At the expected level of impact, the resultant influence on commercial fishing activities from proposed Lease Sale 207 would be negligible and indistinguishable from variations due to natural causes. As a result, there would be very little impact on commercial fishing. Proposed Lease Sale 207 is expected to result in less than a 1 percent change in activities, in pounds landed, or in the value of landings. It will require less than 6 months for fishing activity to recover from any impacts.

A search was conducted for new information published since completion of the Multisale EIS. A search of Internet information sources (including scientific journals) as well as interviews with personnel from academic institutions and governmental resource agencies was conducted to determine availability of new information. Some recent reports (USDOC, NMFS, 2007b and 2007c) have further documented impacts from the 2005 hurricanes on fish and fishery habitat discussed above under "Fish Resources and Essential Fish Habitat" (**Chapter 4.2.8**).

In July 2007, NMFS published a preliminary report for 2006 on U.S. commercial and recreational fisheries (USDOC, NMFS, 2007d). **Table 4** shows the change in commercial landings from 2005 to 2006 for the Gulf of Mexico and the Gulf States. Despite Louisiana's drop in number of landings following Hurricane Katrina, Louisiana still remains the leader in Gulf landings, followed by Mississippi, Texas, Florida (West Coast), and Alabama. Kirkham (2007) states "though the migration into other state waters is not new, the post-storm NOAA statistics suggest a new trend: Fishers are taking more seafood from Louisiana waters than what is brought in to Louisiana ports" and "whether the trends will continue is up for debate. As docks, ramps, and icehouses in Louisiana come back online -- about 85 percent are back, according to a recent Wildlife and Fisheries report -- fishers will be able to bring their catch back to pre-storm ports and buyers" (Louisiana Department of Wildlife and Fisheries, 2007).

The MMS has reexamined the analysis for commercial fishing presented in the Multisale EIS, based on the additional information presented above. No new significant information was discovered that would alter the impact conclusion for commercial fishing presented in the Multisale EIS; therefore, a new analysis of the potential impacts of proposed Lease Sale 207 on commercial fishing is not required. The analysis and potential impacts detailed in the Multisale EIS still apply for proposed Lease Sale 207.

Table 4

U.S. Domestic Landings for the Gulf of Mexico and Gulf States, 2005 and 2006

	2005 (thousand pounds)	2006 (thousand pounds)	Change	2005 (thousand dollars)	2006 (thousand dollars)	Change
Gulf of Mexico	1,196,355	1,285,691	7%	620,987	662,938	7%
Florida, West Coast	70,230	68,913	-2%	132,781	194,023	46%
Alabama	24,032	34,052	42%	39,888	48,566	22%
Mississippi	167,609	221,838	32%	23,386	21,751	-7%
Louisiana	850,194	844,027	-1%	252,596	201,742	-20%
Texas	84,289	116,860	39%	172,337	196,856	14%

Source: USDOC, NMFS, 2007d.

4.2.10. Recreational Fishing

The description of the environment for recreational fishing is in Chapter 3.3.2 of the Multisale EIS. Detailed analysis of the routine, accidental, and cumulative impacts of proposed Lease Sale 207 on recreational fishing is in Chapters 4.2.1.1.10, 4.4.11, and 4.5.12, respectively. The following is a summary of the impact analysis from the Multisale EIS.

With respect to routine events, the development of oil and gas in the proposed lease sale area could attract additional recreational fishing activity to structures installed on productive leases. Each structure placed in the GOM to produce oil or gas would function as a *de facto* artificial reef, attract sport fish, and improve fishing prospects in the immediate vicinity of platforms. This impact would last for the life of the structure until it is removed from the marine environment. Proposed Lease Sale 207 would therefore have a beneficial effect on offshore and deep-sea recreational fishing within developed leases accessible to fishermen. Short-term, space-use conflict could occur during the time that any pipeline is being installed. Impacts on recreational fishing because of OCS-related vessel wakes would be minor because, on average, vessel use associated with proposed Lease Sale 207 would represent less than 1 percent of total vessel use.

With respect to accidental events, the estimated number and size of potential spills associated with proposed Lease Sale 207's activities (Chapter 4.3.1.2 of the Multisale EIS) are unlikely to decrease recreational fishing activity but may divert the location or timing of a few planned fishing trips. Potential impacts on recreational fisheries due to accidental events as a result of proposed Lease Sale 207 would be minor to moderate. Based on the sizes of oil spills assumed for proposed Lease Sale 207, only localized and short-term disruption of recreational fishing activity might result (minor impact).

With respect to cumulative events, recreational fishing continues to be a popular nearshore and offshore recreational activity in the northeastern and central GOM. Concern for the sustainability of fish resources and marine recreational fishing has led to Federal legislation that established a fisheries management process that will include the identification and protection of EFH. The incremental contributions of proposed Lease Sale 207 (as analyzed in Chapter 4.2.1.1.10 in the Multisale EIS) to the cumulative impact on recreational fishing is positive, although minor due to the relatively small number of structures projected for the next 40 years. The cumulative impact of OCS and State oil and gas activities and import tanker spills would be minor. Implementation of proposed Lease Sale 207 would attract some private and charter-boat recreational fishermen farther offshore to the vicinity of the developed lease blocks in pursuit of targeted species known to be associated with petroleum structures in deep water.

A search was conducted for new information published since completion of the Multisale EIS. Research of recreational fishing revealed the following new information. The NMFS has published the preliminary 2006 Marine Recreational Fisheries Statistics Survey (MRFSS) (USDOC, NMFS, 2007e). In 2006, 3.6 million residents participated in marine recreational fishing. All participants, including visitors, took nearly 25 million trips and caught almost 193 million fish. About 65 percent of the trips were made in west Florida, followed by 18 percent in Louisiana, almost 9 percent in Alabama, over 4 percent in Texas, and 4 percent in Mississippi.

The MRFSS is the primary source for marine recreational fisheries data in U.S. waters. This survey combines random telephone interviews and onsite intercept surveys of anglers to estimate recreational catch and effort for inland, State, and Federal waters. In the GOM, surveys are conducted in western Florida, Alabama, Mississippi, and Louisiana. The Texas Parks and Wildlife Department conducts separate surveys that are not directly comparable with NOAA surveys. Texas Parks and Wildlife (Mark Fisher, personal communication, 2008) reported that in 2006 (2007 data is not yet available), approximately 37,492 anglers participated in marine recreational fishing for a total of nearly 6.5 million hours. Of this number, 1,801 anglers (4.8%) participated in fishing in the EEZ. The total number of hours reported for anglers in the EEZ was slightly over 65,000. Most of the fishermen, 33,060' fished on private trips with 4,432 on charter trips.

The most abundant species landed overall was the spotted seatrout with over 1 million fish caught. The second most abundant caught overall was the red drum (266,193 total) followed by the Atlantic croaker (95,676 total). The most common species caught in he EEZ was the red snapper (61,819 total) followed by the king mackerel (25,859 total) and dolphinfish (11,378 total).

Tables 3-12, 3-13, and 3-14 of the Multisale EIS show MRFSS GOM data for 2005, while **Tables 5-7** show MRFSS GOM data for 2006 (USDOC, NMFS, 2007e).

Table 5

Top Species Commonly Caught by Recreational Fishers
in the Marine Recreational Fisheries Statistics Gulf Coast States (except Texas) (2006)

Species	Total All Fish (#)	Total All Fish (lbs)	Inland (#)	Inland (lbs)	Ocean (#)	Ocean (lbs)
Black drum	1,267,386	2,480,078	1,219,109	2,351,043	48,277	129,035
Dolphins	81,400	188,130	870		80,530	188,130
Gray snapper	2,594,974	1,381,957	2,043,579	483,753	551,395	898,204
Greater amberjack	66,394	683,364	1,850		64,544	683,364
Herrings	41,716,268	152,455	41,255,403	152,455	460,865	0
King mackerel	498,355	1,349,952	362,809	590,059	135,546	759,893
Mycteroperca groupers	644,735	231,395	603,463	110,062	41,272	121,333
Pinfishes	6,736,540	369,738	5,710,573	346,356	1,025,967	23,382
Red drum	8,596,876	13,576,884	8,116,594	12,063,913	480,282	1,512,971
Red snapper	1,586,841	1,485,529	62,979	33,287	1,523,862	1,452,242
Saltwater catfishes	8,773,173	862,261	7,673,254	742,800	1,099,919	119,461
Sand seatrout	3,457,656	1,237,721	3,337,144	1,180,793	120,512	56,928
Sheepshead	2,403,692	3,236,779	2,133,947	2,429,966	269,745	806,813
Spotted seatrout	30,439,521	15,500,347	29,925,279	15,196,037	514,242	304,310

Source: USDOC, NMFS, 2007e.

Table 6

Recreational Fishing Participation
in the Marine Recreational Fisheries Statistics Gulf Coast States (2006)

State	Participation Estimate (number of people)			
	Coastal	Non-Coastal	Out-of-State	Total
West Florida	2,083,835		1,988,445	4,072,281
Alabama	232,799	183,511	319,720	736,030
Mississippi	143,417	23,382	26,532	193,331
Louisiana	867,742	108,491	197,841	1,174,074
Gulf Total	3,327,793	315,384	2,532,538	6,175,716

Source: USDOC, NMFS, 2007e.

Table 7

Mode of Fishing in the Marine Recreational Fisheries Statistics Gulf Coast
States (except Texas) 2006

State	Area	Number of Trips	% of State Total
Alabama	Shore Ocean (≤3 mi)	836,479	39
	Shore Inland	372,368	17
	Charter Ocean (≤3 mi)	6,238	0
	Charter Ocean (>3 mi)	61,894	3
	Charter Inland	9,294	0
	Private/Rental Ocean (≤3 mi)	253,917	12
	Private/Rental Ocean (>3 mi)	184,991	9
	Private/Rental Inland	418,244	20
	Total	2,143,425	
West Florida	Shore Ocean (≤3 mi)	3,542,065	22
	Shore Inland	3,195,967	19
	Charter Ocean (≤3 mi)	172,528	1
	Charter Ocean (>3 mi)	268,956	2
	Charter Inland	118,440	1
	Private/Rental Ocean (≤3 mi)	3,654,698	23
	Private/Rental Ocean (>3 mi)	1,015,560	6
	Private/Rental Inland	4,262,060	26
	Total	16,230,274	
Louisiana	Shore Ocean (≤3 mi)	96,247	2
	Shore Inland	837,514	19
	Charter Ocean (≤3 mi)	11,845	0
	Charter Ocean (>3 mi)	56,052	1
	Charter Inland	108,181	2
	Private/Rental Ocean (≤3 mi)	166,798	4
	Private/Rental Ocean (>3 mi)	120,391	3
	Private/Rental Inland	3,094,252	69
	Total	4,491,280	
Mississippi	Shore Ocean (≤3 mi)	727	0
	Shore Inland	324,295	32
	Charter Ocean (≤3 mi)	3,928	0
	Charter Ocean (>3 mi)	68	0
	Charter Inland	3,058	0
	Private/Rental Ocean (≤3 mi)	25,895	3
	Private/Rental Ocean (>3 mi)	29,518	3
	Private/Rental Inland	610,422	61
	Total	997,911	
Gulf Total	Shore Ocean (≤3 mi)	4,475,518	19
	Shore Inland	4,730,144	20
	Charter Ocean (≤3 mi)	194,539	1
	Charter Ocean (>3 mi)	386,970	2
	Charter Inland	238,973	1
	Private/Rental Ocean (≤3 mi)	4,101,308	17
	Private/Rental Ocean (>3 mi)	1,350,460	6
	Private/Rental Inland	8,384,978	35
Total		23,862,890	

Source: USDOC, NMFS, 2007f.

The top species commonly caught by recreational fishers in the MRFSS Gulf Coast States are illustrated in **Table 5**. By number, herring and spotted sea trout, both inland species, were the most common fish caught by recreational anglers in the GOM during 2005 and 2006. In 2006, the estimated catch for herrings was over 41 million fish, up from 24 million in 2005; while anglers caught over 30 million spotted sea trout, up from 23 million in 2005. Other important inland species include red drum, saltwater catfishes, and pinfishes. In offshore oceanic waters of the GOM, the most important species in terms of pounds caught were red drum, red snapper, and sheepshead.

Hurricanes Katrina and Rita impacted recreational fishing from the Florida Panhandle to the Texas border, with additional impacts felt in southern Florida. The hurricanes had a major impact on the supporting infrastructure that anglers require to go fishing (e.g., bait shops, docks and marinas, lodging, fuel and ice facilities, etc.). In addition to damages to boats and facilities, revenue losses associated with lost markets of products or services are occurring. When considered on a regional basis, these lost market channels constitute a considerable reduction in the levels of economic activity, income generation, employment creation, and tax collections.

Storm-related recreational fisheries losses over the next year could total $421 million at the retail level (Louisiana Dept. of Wildlife and Fisheries, 2007). This figure includes losses incurred by licensed charter and guide vessels operating in the severely affected parishes.

In addition, Hurricanes Katrina and Rita deposited extensive amounts of debris over various areas of the Gulf Coast (USDOC, NOAA, 2007). Submerged marine debris poses a hazard to vessel traffic. The NOAA is conducting underwater surveys off the coasts of Louisiana, Mississippi, and Alabama. This information is being used by State and Federal agencies tasked with removing marine debris left by Hurricane Katrina, and it will aid in planning for the aftermath of future storms.

The MMS has reexamined the analysis for recreational fishing presented in the Multisale EIS, based on the additional information presented above. No new significant information was discovered that would alter the impact conclusion for recreational fishing presented in the Multisale EIS; therefore, a new analysis of the potential impacts of proposed Lease Sale 207 on recreational fishing is not required. The analysis and potential impacts detailed in the Multisale EIS still apply for proposed Lease Sale 207.

4.2.11. Recreational Resources

The description of the environment for recreational resources can be found in Chapter 3.3.3 of the Multisale EIS. Detailed analysis of the routine, accidental, and cumulative impacts of proposed Lease Sale 207 on recreational resources can be found in Chapters 4.2.1.1.11, 4.4.12, and 4.5.13, respectively. The following is a summary of the impact analysis from the Multisale EIS.

The northern GOM coastal zone is one of the major recreational regions of the U.S., particularly in connection with marine fishing and beach-related activities. The coastal beaches, barrier islands, estuarine bays and sounds, river deltas, and tidal marshes are used extensively and intensively for recreational activity by residents of the Gulf States and tourists from throughout the Nation, as well as from foreign countries. Commercial and private recreational facilities and establishments (such as resorts and marinas) also serve as primary interest areas and support services for people who seek enjoyment from the recreational resources associated with the GOM.

With respect to routine events, marine debris will be lost from time to time from OCS oil and gas operations resulting from proposed Lease Sale 207. The impact on Gulf Coast recreational beaches is expected to be minimal. The incremental increase in helicopter and vessel traffic is expected to add very little additional noise that may affect beach users. Proposed Lease Sale 207 is expected to result in nearshore operations that may adversely affect the enjoyment of some Gulf Coast beach uses; however, these will have little effect on the number of beach users.

With respect to accidental events, it is unlikely that a spill would be a major threat to recreational beaches because spill sizes are relatively small based on past data and any impacts would be short-term and localized. Should a spill contact a recreational beach, it would be in a degraded state from weathering processes that had acted upon it, and short-term displacement of recreational activity from the areas directly contacted by a spill would occur. Beaches directly impacted would be expected to close for periods of 2-6 weeks or until the cleanup operations were complete. Should a spill result in a large volume of oil contacting a beach or a large recreational area being contacted by an oil slick, visitation to the area could be reduced by as much as 5-15 percent for as long as one summer season, but such an event should have no long-term effect on tourism. Tarballs can lessen the enjoyment of the recreational beaches but should have no long-term effect on the overall use of beaches.

With respect to cumulative events, debris and litter derived from both offshore and onshore sources are likely to diminish the attractiveness of beaches and degrade the ambience of shoreline recreational activities, thereby negatively affecting the experience of using recreational beaches in the WPA. The incremental beach trash resulting from proposed Lease Sale 207 is expected to be minimal. Mitigation measures for oil and gas operator's trash and debris handling and labeling requirements for equipment are effective at minimizing OCS trash and debris from entering the water. Platforms and drilling rigs operating nearshore may affect the ambience of recreational beaches, especially beach wilderness areas. The sound, sight, and wakes of OCS-related and non-OCS-related vessels, as well as OCS helicopters and other light aircraft traffic, are occasional distractions that are noticed by some beach users. Oil that contacts the coast may preclude short-term recreational use of one or more Gulf Coast beaches at the park or community levels. Displacement of recreational use from impacted areas will occur, and a short-term decline in tourism may result. Beach use at the regional level is unlikely to change from normal patterns; however, closure of specific beaches or parks directly impacted by a large oil spill is likely during cleanup operations. The incremental contributions of proposed Lease Sale 207 (as analyzed in Chapter 4.2.1.1.11 of the Multisale EIS) to the cumulative impact on recreational resources is minor due to the limited effect of increased helicopter, vessel traffic, and marine debris on the number of beach users.

A search was conducted for new information published since completion of the Multisale EIS. An Internet search of available literature was performed, including Federal and State agencies and industry websites. Research revealed the following new information.

Recreation and tourism are major sources of employment along the Gulf Coast. **Table 8** presents employment in tourism-related industries in 2005 compiled from travel- and tourism-related industries in the County Business Patterns (USDOC, Bureau of the Census, 2007). Employment data are assumed to be in various travel-related industries, including: food and beverage stores, gas stations, general merchandise stores, passenger air transportation, transit and ground passenger transportation, scenic and sightseeing transportation, passenger car rental, travel arrangement and reservation services, arts/entertainment/recreation, and overnight accommodation and food services. The data are only for coastal counties and parishes because they potentially are affected by routine events, such as OCS-related air and vessel traffic, and accidental events, such as oil spills. This is different from the data for all counties and parishes in Labor Market Areas (LMA's) and Economic Impact Areas (EIA's) in Tables 3-15 and 3-16 in the Multisale EIS. The LMA's and EIA's extend inland geographically including inland counties and parishes not economically linked to the tourism and recreation of coastal counties. The data in **Table 8** more correctly describes the level of tourism-related employment and establishments potentially affected by OCS activities.

Beach visitation in Louisiana is low compared with other Gulf Coast States. Gambling is one of the most popular activities for nonresident visitors to Louisiana. In 2004, approximately 21 percent of nonresident visitors gambled on their trip to the State (Travel Industry Association of America, 2003-2005), down from 25 percent in 2002 and 23 percent in 2003.

There are 16 casinos in Louisiana (14 riverboats, 1 land-based, and 1 racetrack), several of which are located along Louisiana's coast in Lake Charles, Houma, and the New Orleans metropolitan area. The casinos generated a gross revenue of $2.57 billion and tax revenue of $528 million, with a visitor volume of over 36 million in 2006 (American Gaming Association, 2007). In 2003 the industry employed approximately 18,329 workers, admitted 37.5 million visitors, and generated nearly $2 billion in gross revenues and $414.2 million in taxes (American Gaming Association, 2003), reflecting pre-Katrina activity. Taxes are allocated among the general fund, the City of New Orleans, public retirement systems, State Capitol improvements, and a rainy day fund.

During the 2005 hurricane season, Hurricanes Katrina and Rita inflicted severe damage on the Gulf Coast and deposited extensive amounts of debris over various areas of the Gulf Coast (USDOC, NOAA, 2007). Submerged marine debris poses a hazard to vessel traffic. The NOAA is conducting underwater surveys off the coasts of Louisiana, Mississippi, and Alabama. This information is being used by State and Federal agencies involved with removing marine debris left by Hurricane Katrina and will aid in planning for the aftermath of future storms.

Table 8

Employment and Establishments in Tourism Related Industries in 2005 by Coastal County and Parish

Area	Employment	Establishments	Area	Employment	Establishments
Texas			**Alabama**		
Cameron	20,192	1,046	Baldwin	13,084	690
Willacy	543	56	Mobile	26,101	1,322
Aransas	843	118	Alabama Total	39,185	2,012
Kenedy	10	1			
Kleberg	1,932	114	**Florida**		
Nueces	24,000	1,281	Bay	14,651	846
Refugio	414	22	Franklin	963	82
San Patricio	3,876	224	Gulf	561	51
Brazoria	12,962	686	Escambia	20,783	965
Matagorda	1,750	159	Okaloosa	17,768	824
Calhoun	1,148	94	Santa Rosa	6,569	321
Jackson	682	48	Walton	4,061	206
Jefferson	15,689	830	Jefferson	527	49
Chambers	1,205	896	Wakulla	849	68
Galveston	20,085	1,010	Taylor	1,118	80
Harris	253,614	11,700	Citrus	5,937	359
Texas Total	358,945	18,285	Dixie	378	46
			Levy	2,297	151
Louisiana			Hernando	8,283	388
Cameron	326	29	Hillsborough	92,467	3,678
Iberia	5,330	213	Pasco	19,798	1,016
Vermillion	1,996	158	Pinellas	68,259	3,568
Lafourche	5,391	299	Collier	30,501	1,191
St. Mary	4,622	201	Lee	43,592	1,860
Terrebonne	8,177	412	Miami-Dade	166,316	8,388
Orleans	56,900	1,972	Monroe	15,065	899
Plaquemines	1,317	110	Charlotte	9,126	414
St. Bernard	3,409	210	Manatee	17,546	907
St. Tammany	15,115	755	Sarasota	28,374	1,371
Louisiana Total	102,583	4,359	Florida Total	575,789	27,728
Mississippi			**Gulf States Total**	1,113,214	53,920
Hancock	3,623	160			
Harrison	26,209	764			
Jackson	6,880	612			
Mississippi Total	36,712	1,536			

Source: USDOC, Bureau of the Census, 2007.

The Ocean Conservancy sponsors national and international beach cleanups, including annual events in Louisiana, Mississippi, and Alabama. The Louisiana event is coordinated by the Louisiana Department of Environmental Quality (LADEQ), Litter Reduction and Public Action Program. Statistics have not been published for the last Louisiana event, held on September 15, 2006 (LADEQ, 2007b). The 2007 beach sweep event was also held on September 15.

Clean Marina Programs encourage recreational boaters and marina owners to protect coastal water quality by using environmentally sound operating and maintenance procedures. In the Texas program, 28 percent of the State's 356 inland and coastal marinas are participating, with 59 being certified as clean marinas. Certification is achieved by reducing harmful chemicals and trash and debris having the potential to enter the water, and by reducing excess nutrients in the water through proper waste-handling practices using up-to-date equipment (Texas Sea Grant, 2006).

The 1999-2000 National Survey on Recreation and the Environment (NSRE) is the first national survey to include a broad assessment of the Nation's participation in marine recreation (USDOC, NMFS, 2005). The Multisale EIS presented data from the 2001 National Survey of Fishing, Hunting, and Wildlife-Associated Recreation for the five Gulf States (USDOI, FWS and USDOC, Bureau of the Census, 2001). The 2006 survey used a methodology similar to the 2001 survey. The 2006 survey began in March with the U.S. Census Bureau's initial interviews of people in 85,000 households to identify a representative sample of 31,500 anglers and hunters and 24,300 wildlife watchers for interviews, primarily by phone, about their activities. The 2006 survey findings were released in November 2007 (USDOI, FWS, 2007d) and are summarized in **Table 9**.

Table 9

Participation in Wildlife-Associated Recreation by State Residents
Inside and Outside Their Resident State: 2006

State of Residence	Population	Total Participants		Sportspersons		Wildlife-Watching Participants	
		Number	Percent Population	Number	Percent Population	Number	Percent Population
Louisiana	3,433	1,106	32	678	20	712	21
Texas	17,076	5,481	32	2,668	16	4,111	24

All numbers in thousands.

The MMS has reexamined the analysis for recreational resources presented in the Multisale EIS, based on the additional information presented above. No new significant information was discovered that would alter the impact conclusion for recreational resources presented in the Multisale EIS; therefore, a new analysis of the potential impacts of proposed Lease Sale 207 on recreational resources is not required. The analysis and potential impacts detailed in the Multisale EIS still apply for proposed Lease Sale 207.

4.2.12. Archaeological Resources

Archaeological resources are any material remains of human life or activities that are at least 50 years of age and that are of archaeological interest (30 CFR 250.105). The Archaeological Resources Regulation (30 CFR 250.194) provides specific authority to each MMS Regional Director to require archaeological resource surveys, analyses, and reports. Surveys are required prior to any exploration or development activities on leases within areas determined to have a high potential for archaeological resources (NTL's 2005-G07 and 2006-G07).

The description of archaeological resources (prehistoric and historic) can be found in Chapter 3.3.4 of the Multisale EIS. A detailed impact analysis of the routine, accidental, and cumulative impacts of proposed Lease Sale 207 on archaeological resources can be found in Chapters 4.2.1.1.12, 4.4.14, and 4.5.14 of the Multisale EIS, respectively. The following information is a summary of the impact analysis incorporated from the Multisale EIS.

The greatest potential impact on archaeological resources as a result of proposed Lease Sale 207 would result from direct contact between an offshore activity (platform installation, drilling rig installation or pipeline emplacement, or dredging) and a prehistoric site located on the continental shelf or an historic shipwreck. The NTL for archaeological resource surveys in the GOM Region, NTL 2005-G07, specifies a 300-m linespacing for areas having the potential for containing prehistoric sites on the continental shelf, 50-m linespacing for remote-sensing surveys of leases within the areas having high potential for historic shipwrecks in water depths ≤200 m (656 ft), and 300-m linespacing of leases within the areas having high potential for historic shipwrecks in water depths >200 m (656 ft). NTL 2006-G07 identifies those lease blocks that have been designated as having a high potential for containing archaeological resources.

The archaeological survey and archaeological clearance of sites required before beginning oil and gas activities on a lease are expected to be highly effective at identifying possible archaeological resources. Since the survey and clearance provide a significant reduction in the potential for a damaging interaction between an impact-producing factor and an archaeological resource, there is a very small possibility of an

OCS activity contacting an archaeological resource. Should such contact occur, there would be damage to or loss of significant and/or unique archaeological information. The effect of OCS-generated debris swept from platforms during storms is a potential complicating factor for MMS analysts examining the sea bottom for ferromagnetic debris. Metallic debris can indicate the presence of a target that is not an archaeological resource (false positive). There is, however, still a requirement for the survey before bottom disturbing activities may take place. Targets need to be examined more closely to determine their origin. Other than to cause more complicated analyses of bottom signals that may end up being false positives the effect of debris from OCS infrastructure damaged during storms is not significant. Debris falling within the 1,320 ft (400 m) clearance radius of platforms and the 600 ft (183 m) clearance radius for well protectors and caissons are cleared upon decommissioning, as stated in the guidance provided for site clearance in NTL 98-26.

Spills, collisions, and blowouts are accidental events that can happen in association with a proposed activity in the Lease Sale 207 area. If an accidental event occurs as a result of one of these events, there could be an impact on archaeological resources. Oil spills have the potential to affect both prehistoric and historic archaeological resources. Impacts on historic resources would be limited to visual impacts and possibly physical impacts associated with spill cleanup operations. Impacts on prehistoric archaeological sites would be the result of hydrocarbon contamination of organic materials, which have the potential to date site occupation through radiocarbon dating techniques, as well as possible physical disturbance associated with spill cleanup operations. Since archaeological sites are protected under law, it is expected that any spill cleanup operations would be conducted in such a way as to cause little or no impacts on archaeological resources. Visual impacts on coastal historic sites would be temporary and reversible; however, should an oil spill directly contact a coastal prehistoric site, unique or significant archaeological information could be lost, and this impact would be irreversible.

The cumulative analysis considers the effects of impact-producing factors related to Lease Sale 207. Those activities in the cumulative activity area include: trawling, sport diving, commercial treasure hunting, seismic exploration in State waters, and tropical storms on archaeological resources. Specific types of impact-producing factors associated with OCS activities that are considered in this analysis include drilling rig and platform emplacement, pipeline emplacement, anchoring, oil spills, dredging, new onshore facilities, and ferromagnetic debris. Archaeological surveys are assumed to be highly effective in reducing the potential for an interaction between an impact-producing activity and archaeological resources. Other users of the OCS, such as trawl fishers, may encounter snags and net losses from debris. There are, however, remedies available to commercial fishermen who can demonstrate their loss was due to OCS activity.

Onshore development associated with activities from proposed Lease Sale 207 could result in the direct physical contact between the construction of new onshore facilities or pipeline canals and previously unidentified historic or prehistoric sites. Direct physical contact with a historic site could cause physical damage to, or complete destruction of, information on the history of the region and the Nation. Direct physical contact with a prehistoric site could destroy fragile artifacts or site features and could disturb the archaeological context of the site. The result would be the loss of information on the prehistory of North America and the Gulf Coast region. Facilities that are projected to be constructed onshore as a result of proposed Lease Sale 207 must receive approval from the pertinent Federal, State, county/parish, and/or communities before construction may proceed. Protection of archaeological resources in these cases is expected to be achieved through the various approval processes involved. There is, therefore, no expected impact on historic or prehistoric sites that support Lease Sale 207 from onshore development.

Recent hurricane activity in the GOM is certain to have impacted archaeological resources in shallow water. A search was conducted for new information published since completion of the Multisale EIS; however, little new information was identified. Yet, it is almost certain that any shipwrecks within the path of Hurricanes Katrina or Rita in shallow water were impacted to some extent by these storms. In September 2005 the National Park Service (NPS) conducted a study of sites along the Gulf Coast that were impacted by Hurricane Katrina (USDOI, NPS, 2005). This assessment identified three types of damage that can occur to archaeological sites: tree throws; storm surge, scouring and erosion; and seabed shifting. On the OCS, the two primary types of damage would be associated with storm surge and seabed shifting. Damage from either of these activities could adversely affect both prehistoric and historic sites on the OCS.

A recently published report, *Archaeological and Biological Analysis of World War II Shipwrecks in the Gulf of Mexico: Artificial Reef Effect in Deep Water* (Church et al., 2007), documents the results of a multidisciplinary study that focused on the biological and archaeological aspects of seven World War II era shipwrecks in the north-central portion of the Gulf of Mexico. The study was funded by MMS and NOAA's Office of Ocean Exploration.

Seven shipwrecks, including a German Type II U-boat submarine and some of its targets, were investigated. The ships lie in water ranging from 122 to 1,981 m (400 to 6,500 ft) deep. The study found deep-sea wrecks act as artificial reefs, attracting far more species of plants and animals than expected. The finding indicates that oil and gas production platforms in deep water are likely to serve as hard surface, supporting hundreds of life forms.

Wrecks in moderate depths gave researchers clear evidence of many rare and uncommon invertebrate species in close proximity to the wrecks and on the wrecks themselves. The number of species and individuals declined rapidly in proportion to distance away from the wrecks, showing that these wrecks form an attractive habitat for many kinds of marine life. Wrecks at these intermediate depths had 50 percent more species than those in shallower water or deeper water. Shallower water wrecks, likely because of turbidity, and deeper water wrecks because of the extreme conditions of cold, darkness, and pressure, hosted a smaller number of species.

The scientists reported, among other findings, that the diversity of fish species generally decreases with depth. At the shallower water wrecks, where corals were growing, reef fishes were present. At the deepest water wrecks, below the photic zone of approximately 200 m (656 ft), no corals were found nor were community structure and fish density significantly different over the wrecks as opposed to away from them. Therefore, scientists conclude that, in the deepest water, the upper levels of bottom-founded or floating offshore platforms will attract considerable marine life, but the platforms are not likely to attract fish at their deepest levels. The marine archaeology part of the study positively confirmed the identity of three wrecks and found a relationship among water depth, ship size, and the size of the debris field. The state of preservation of the wrecks was correlated with water depth. No wreck was found to be contaminating or adversely affecting the area around them.

The MMS recently awarded a study to investigate the impacts that recent storm activity may have had on historic shipwrecks in the Gulf of Mexico. Remote-sensing surveys for this study were completed in May 2007 and dive operations were carried out in October 2007 with a final report of findings expected early in 2009 (PBS&J, in preparation). Preliminary analysis of the remote-sensing surveys indicates that at least 3 of the 10 shipwrecks examined were affected by recent storm activity.

The MMS has reexamined the analysis for archaeological resources presented in the Multisale EIS, based on the additional information presented above. No new significant information was discovered that would alter the impact conclusion for archaeological resources presented in the Multisale EIS; therefore, a new analysis of the potential impacts of proposed Lease Sale 207 on archaeological resources is not required. The analysis and potential impacts detailed in the Multisale EIS still apply for proposed Lease Sale 207.

4.2.13. Human Resources and Land Use

4.2.13.1. Land Use and Coastal Infrastructure

Land use and OCS-related coastal infrastructure in the analysis area are discussed in Chapters 3.3.5.1.2 and 3.3.5.8 of the Multisale EIS and include the following: service bases, navigation channels, helicopter hubs, construction facilities, processing facilities, terminals, waste disposal and storage facilities, coastal pipelines, and coastal barging. A detailed impact analysis of the routine, accidental, and cumulative impacts of proposed Lease Sale 207 on land use and coastal infrastructure can be found in Chapters 4.2.1.1.13.1, 4.4.14.1, and 4.5.15.1 of the Multisale EIS, respectively. The following is a summary of the impact analysis incorporated from the Multisale EIS.

Proposed Lease Sale 207 would not require additional coastal infrastructure, with the exception of possibly one new gas processing facility and one new pipeline landfall, and would not alter the current land use of the analysis area. There may be some expansion at current facilities that may also include upgrades and replacement of existing facilities, but the land in the analysis area is sufficient to handle such development and the net land-use footprint would remain approximately the same. There is also sufficient land to construct a new gas processing plant in the analysis area, if necessary in the future.

Accidental events such as oil or chemical spills, blowouts, and vessel collisions would have no effects on land use. Coastal or nearshore spills could have short-term adverse effects on coastal infrastructure requiring clean up of any oil or chemicals spilled.

Activities relating to the OCS Program and State production are expected to minimally affect the analysis area's land use. Land use in the analysis area will evolve over time; most changes are likely to occur as a result of general regional growth rather than activities associated with the OCS Program and State production. Projected new coastal infrastructure by state as a result of the OCS Program is shown in Table 4-9 of the Multisale EIS. While it is possible that up to 14 new, "greenfield" gas processing facilities could be developed, it is much more likely that a large share of the natural gas processing capacity that will be needed by the industry will be located at existing facilities, using future investments for expansions and/or to replace depreciated capital equipment. It is likely that few (if any) new plants would be developed along the CPA or WPA. Any changes to supporting infrastructure (mostly facility expansions, except for the 4-6 new pipeline shore facilities and any new, "greenfield" gas processing plants) are expected to be contained on available land. Most subareas in the analysis area have strong industrial bases and designated industrial parks to accommodate future growth in oil and gas businesses.

As stated in Chapter 4.1.2.1.7 of the Multisale EIS, MMS assumes that most new OCS pipelines will connect to existing pipelines in Federal and State waters, and result in few, if any, new pipeline landfalls. Up to one new pipeline landfall was projected as the result of proposed Lease Sale 207, and 32-47 new pipeline landfalls were projected as a result of the OCS Program from 2007 to 2046. The term "pipeline shore facility" is a broad term describing the onshore location where the first stage of processing occurs for OCS pipelines carrying different combinations of oil, condensate, gas, and produced water. A pipeline shore facility may support one or several pipelines. In Chapter 4.1.2.1.5.1 of the Multisale EIS, no new pipeline shore facilities are projected as a result of proposed Lease Sale 207. As a result of the OCS Program, new shore facilities may be needed to support new larger oil pipeline landfalls. A total of 4-6 new pipeline shore facilities are projected as a result of the OCS Program from 2007 to 2046.

Port Fourchon is expected to experience significant cumulative impacts on its land use from OCS-related expansion. Increased OCS-related usage from port clients, and ancillary business that rely on port clients, such as restaurants, gas stations, and overnight lodging, are expected to significantly impact LA Hwy 1 in Lafourche Parish. A major rebuilding and upgrade of LA Hwy 1 would introduce a group of construction workers into the area for the duration of the construction. Also, increased demand for water by upgraded and expanded OCS port clients, ancillary business, and a temporary worker population for upgrading LA Hwy 1 will further strain Lafourche Parish's water system. It is assumed that the Louisiana Department of Natural Resources' existing procedures to identify potential regulatory and restoration conflicts will continue to be utilized, including current requirements that any project proposed within ¼ mi from either an active or proposed restoration project be reviewed to determine if it would interfere or have adverse effects on the restoration project (USACOE, 2004). Therefore, new coastal infrastructure that may result from proposed Lease Sale 207 or the OCS Program would not interfere with active or proposed restoration projects.

The MMS recently analyzed historical data to validate past scenario projections, including projects involving new pipeline landfalls (USDOI, MMS, 2007e). This analysis confirms MMS's assumption that the majority of new pipelines constructed would connect to the existing infrastructure in Federal and State waters and that very few would result in new pipeline landfalls. Most pipeline landfalls in the GOM transport production resulting from more than one lease sale; therefore, an OCS pipeline landfall could rarely be attributed only to a single lease sale. Multiple factors have influenced the decrease in the number of new pipeline landfalls. Therefore, MMS's projection of up to one new pipeline landfall per lease sale may be too high. Although there will be some instances where new pipelines may need to be constructed, there is nothing to suggest any dramatic shifts would be expected in trends for new landfalls given the current outlook for GOM development, particularly in coastal Louisiana.

The MMS has reexamined the analysis for land use and coastal infrastructure presented in the Multisale EIS, based on the additional information presented above. No new significant information was discovered that would alter the impact conclusion for land use and coastal infrastructure presented in the Multisale EIS; therefore, a new analysis of the potential impacts of proposed Lease Sale 207 on land use and coastal infrastructure is not required. The analysis and potential impacts detailed in the Multisale EIS still apply for proposed Lease Sale 207.

4.2.13.2. Demographics

The description of the environment for demographics is described in Chapter 3.3.5.4 of the Multisale EIS. Detailed analysis of the routine, accidental, and cumulative impacts of proposed Lease Sale 207 on demographics is presented in Chapters 4.2.1.1.13.2, 4.4.14.2, and 4.5.15.2 of the Multisale EIS, respectively. The following is a summary of the impact analysis from the Multisale EIS.

Routine activities relating to proposed Lease Sale 207 are expected to affect minimally the analysis area's land use, infrastructure, and demography. These impacts are projected to mirror employment effects that are estimated to be negligible to any one EIA (**Figure 8**). Baseline patterns and distributions of these factors, as described in Chapter 3.3.5.4 of the Multisale EIS, are expected to approximately maintain the same level. Changes in land use throughout the analysis area are expected to be contained and minimal. The OCS-related infrastructure is in place and will not change as a result of proposed Lease Sale 207. Current baseline estimates of population growth for the analysis area show a continuation of growth, but at a slower rate.

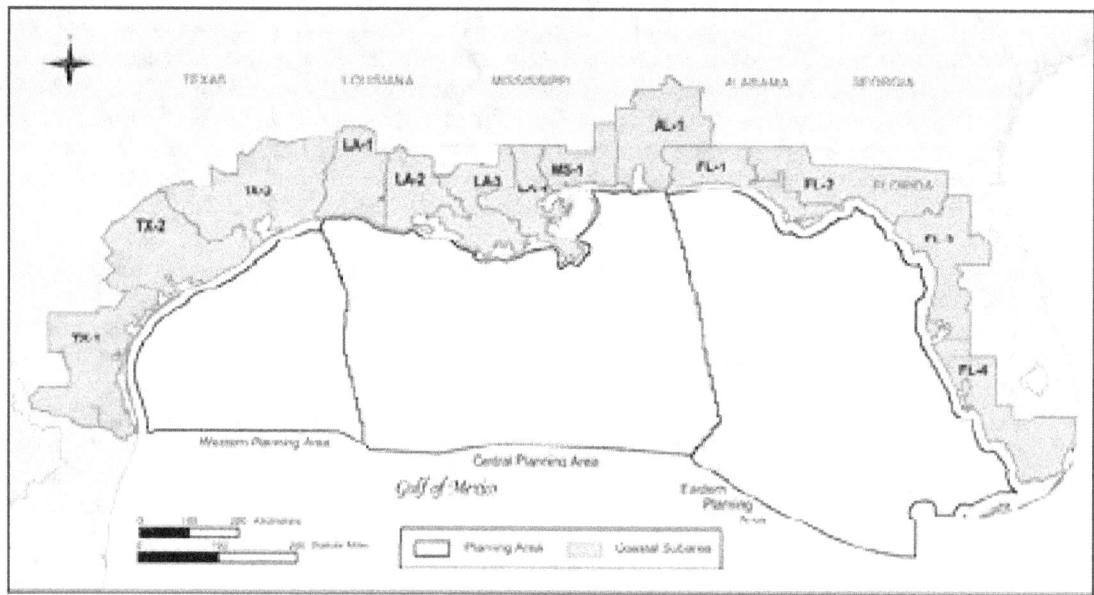

Figure 8.   Economic Impact Areas in the Northern Gulf of Mexico.

Accidental events associated with proposed Lease Sale 207, such as oil or chemical spills, blowouts, and vessel collisions, would have no effects on the demographic characteristics of the Gulf coastal communities.

The cumulative effects of human and natural activities in the coastal area have severely degraded the deltaic processes of sediment replenishment and, on the delta plain, have shifted the coastal area of Louisiana from a condition of net land building to one of net landloss. As inland marshes and barrier islands erode or subside, without effective restoration efforts, the population in coastal communities in southern Louisiana is expected to shift to the more northern portions of parishes bordering the ocean and cause the populations in urban and suburban areas to increase and those in rural coastal areas to decline (USACOE, 2004).

Cumulative activities related to the OCS Program are expected to affect minimally the analysis area's demography. Baseline patterns and distributions of these factors, as described in Chapter 3.3.5.4.1 of the Multisale EIS, are not expected to change for the analysis area as a whole. The baseline population patterns are expected to change for the eight counties and parishes that were most negatively affected by the 2005 hurricane season (see Chapter 3.3.5.4 of the Multisale EIS for a discussion of these changes). Some regions within Louisiana EIA's, Port Fourchon in particular, are expected to experience some impacts from increased population and demand on utilities and the education system as a result of an expanded labor force supporting OCS activity. As discussed in Chapter 4.2.1.1.13.2 of the Multisale EIS, proposed Lease Sale 207 is expected have an incremental contribution of less than 1 percent to the population level in any of the EIA's. Given the low level of population growth and industrial expansion associated with proposed Lease Sale 207, the baseline age and racial distribution pattern and educational status of people living in the impact area is expected to continue through the year 2046.

In the Multisale EIS, MMS used data from Woods & Poole's *Complete Economic and Demographic Data Source* (Woods & Poole Economics, Inc., 2006) for baseline population and employment estimates over the 40-year life of a typical proposed WPA lease sale. The 2007 Woods & Poole data became available in late August 2007 and contains their revised estimates regarding the economic and demographic impacts of the 2005 hurricanes on the Gulf region (Woods & Poole Economics, Inc., 2007). In the new data, population, income, and employment were assumed to decline from 2005 to 2006 by 76 percent in St. Bernard Parish, Louisiana; 51 percent in Orleans Parish, Louisiana; 22 percent in Plaquemines Parish, Louisiana; 19 percent in Cameron Parish, Louisiana; 13 percent in Hancock County, Mississippi; and 11 percent in Harrison County, Mississippi. In each case, these losses were less than those that were assumed in the Woods & Poole 2006 data. The 2007 data also have revised assumptions regarding counties and parishes that experienced population and employment gains because of Hurricane Katrina displacement: 9 percent in Pearl River County, Mississippi; 7 percent in Tangipahoa Parish, Louisiana; 5 percent in St. John the Baptist Parish, Louisiana; 5 percent in East Baton Rouge Parish, Louisiana; and 4 percent in St. Charles Parish, Louisiana from 2005 to 2006. In each case, these gains were less than those that were assumed in the 2006 data.

As discussed in **Chapter 4.1.1**, the exploration and development activity scenarios used in the Multisale EIS for a typical WPA sale remain unchanged and are used for the analysis of proposed Lease Sale 207. Consequently, the population projections for a typical proposed WPA sale in Table 4-28 of the Multisale EIS are unchanged for proposed Lease Sale 207. The MMS reanalyzed the high-case population impacts on a percentage basis for the three EIA's that exhibited the highest impacts in the Multisale EIS (LA-2, LA-3, and LA-4) using the revised Woods & Poole data. With the exception of year 1 (2008) for LA-4, which declined slightly, the population impacts on a percentage basis for the three EIA's are the same as reported in Table 4-29 of the Multisale EIS. Thus, the potential population impacts described in the Multisale EIS and summarized above apply for proposed Lease Sale 207. The MMS reanalyzed the population impacts on a percentage basis for all of the EIA's using the revised Woods & Poole data; however, only the results for EIA's LA-2, LA-3, and LA-4 changed on a percentage basis. The maximum population impacts on a percentage basis for the three EIA's are the same as reported in Table 4-29 of the Multisale EIS. Thus, the potential population impacts described in the Multisale EIS and summarized above apply for proposed Lease Sale 207.

A search was conducted for new information published since completion of the Multisale EIS. Research of all references for demographics in the Multisale EIS revealed the following new information. The following information is summarized from Rowley (2007). The Louisiana Public Health Institute (LPHI) estimated the City of New Orleans's population at 191,139 in January 2007, the U.S. Census Bureau estimated the population at 223,388 in July 2006, and the City estimates it closer to 230,000. For St. Bernard Parish, the Census Bureau estimated the population at 66,441 in 2000 and 15,514 in July 2006, and the LPHI estimates it at 25,296 in January 2007.

Hurricane Katrina flooded more than 40 percent of Hancock County, Mississippi. Prior to Hurricane Katrina the Hancock County population was 46,546; as of July 2006, the Census estimated it at 40,421, indicating a substantial return of population. The Jefferson Parish population estimates are 451,049 in 2000, 431,361 in July 2006, and 434,666 in January 2007. The high population in Jefferson Parish indicates an in-migration of former residents of Orleans, St. Bernard, and Plaquemines Parishes and seasonal construction workers. See Chapter 3.3.5.5.1 of the Multisale EIS for the relationship of population to housing availability and employment.

A year and a half after Hurricanes Katrina and Rita, the recovery was uneven throughout the areas originally affected (Rowley, 2007). Areas where the most severe problems remain are New Orleans and St. Bernard Parish, Louisiana; and Hancock County, Mississippi. Recovery is well underway in Jefferson Parish, Lake Charles, and Cameron Parish, Louisiana; and Biloxi, Gulfport, and Pascagoula, Mississippi; and Bayou La Batre, Alabama. Recovery is driving expansion in East Baton Rouge and St. Tammany Parishes, Louisiana; Jackson, Hattiesburg, and Laurel Mississippi; and Gulf Shores and Mobile, Alabama. The measures of recovery are the functions of local government, population, crime, economic and fiscal effects, local government budgets, housing, and labor.

The MMS has reexamined the analysis for demographics presented in the Multisale EIS, based on the additional information presented above. No new significant information was discovered that would alter the impact conclusion for demographics presented in the Multisale EIS; therefore, a new analysis of the potential impacts of proposed Lease Sale 207 on demographics is not required. The analysis and potential impacts detailed in the Multisale EIS still apply for proposed Lease Sale 207.

4.2.13.3. Economic Factors

The description of the current economic factors for the GOM analysis area can be found in Chapter 3.3.5.5 of the Multisale EIS. A detailed impact analysis of the routine, accidental, and cumulative impacts of proposed Lease Sale 207 on economic factors can be found in Chapters 4.2.1.1.13.3, 4.4.14.3, and 4.5.15.3 of the Multisale EIS, respectively. The following is a summary of the impact analysis incorporated from the Multisale EIS.

Should proposed Lease Sale 207 occur, there would be only minor economic changes in the Texas, Louisiana, Mississippi, Alabama, and Florida EIA's (**Figure 5**). Proposed Lease Sale 207 is expected to generate less than a 1 percent increase in employment in any of these subareas. This demand will be met primarily with the existing population and available labor force. Accidental events such as oil or chemical spills, blowouts, and vessel collisions could have modest, short-term adverse economic consequences. Negative, long-term economic and social impacts may be more substantial if fishing, shrimping, oystering, and/or tourism were to suffer or were to be perceived as having suffered because of the event.

The OCS Program will produce only minor economic changes in most of the individual EIA's. However, it is projected to substantially impact the Louisiana EIA's LA-2 and LA-3, with OCS-related employment expected to peak at 23.8 percent and 9.8 percent of total employment, respectively. On a regional level, activities related to the OCS Program are expected to significantly impact employment in Lafourche Parish, Louisiana, within EIA LA-3. Therefore, the population, housing, roads (LA Hwy 1), water supply, schools, and hospitals in the parish will be affected and potentially strained.

A search was conducted for new information published since completion of the Multisale EIS. A search of Internet information sources as well as personal communication with regional and national economic experts was conducted to determine the availability of new information that would affect the impact analyses. In the Multisale EIS, MMS used data from Woods & Poole's *Complete Economic and Demographic Data Source* (Woods & Poole Economics, Inc., 2006) for baseline population and employment estimates over the 40-year life of a typical proposed WPA lease sale. The 2007 Woods & Poole data became available in late August 2007 and contains their revised estimates regarding the economic and demographic impacts of the 2005 hurricanes on the Gulf region (Woods & Poole Economics, Inc., 2007). In the new data, population, income, and employment were assumed to decline from 2005 to 2006 by 76 percent in St. Bernard Parish, Louisiana; 51 percent in Orleans Parish, Louisiana; 22 percent in Plaquemines Parish, Louisiana; 19 percent in Cameron Parish; Louisiana; 13 percent in Hancock County, Mississippi; and 11 percent in Harrison County, Mississippi. In each case, these losses were less than those that were assumed in the Woods & Poole 2006 data. The 2007 data also have revised assumptions regarding counties and parishes that experienced population and employment gains because of Hurricane Katrina displacement: 9 percent in Pearl River County, Mississippi; 7 percent in Tangipahoa Parish, Louisiana; 5 percent in St. John the Baptist Parish, Louisiana; 5 percent in East Baton Rouge Parish, Louisiana; and 4 percent in St. Charles Parish, Louisiana from 2005 to 2006. In each case, these gains were less than those that were assumed in the 2006 data.

As discussed in **Chapter 4.1.1**, the exploration and development activity scenarios used in the Multisale EIS for a typical WPA sale remain unchanged and are used for the analysis of proposed Lease Sale 207. Consequently, the employment projections for a typical proposed WPA sale in the Multisale EIS (Tables 4-30 and 4-31) are unchanged for Lease Sale 207. The MMS reanalyzed the employment impacts on a percentage basis for all of the economic impact areas (EIA's) using the revised Woods & Poole data; however, only the results for EIA's LA-2, LA-3, and LA-4 changed on a percentage basis,. The revised low and high case results are shown in **Table 10**. The maximum employment impacts on a percentage basis for the three EIA's are the same as reported in Table 4-32 of the Multisale EIS (LA-2 ranges from 0.1% to 0.2% and LA-3 and LA-4 are both 0.1% for the low and high cases, respectively). Thus, the potential employment impacts described in the Multisale EIS and summarized above apply for proposed Lease Sale 207.

Table 10

Projected Employment* Associated with Proposed Lease Sale 207 by Economic Impact Area

Calendar Year	Revised Baseline Employment Projections[1]			WPA Proposed Action Employment Estimates[2]						Projected Employment Associated with Proposed Lease Sale 207 as Percent of Total Baseline Employment					
	LA2	LA3	LA4	LA2		LA3		LA4		LA2		LA3		LA4	
	In Thousands			Low	High	Low	High	Low	High	Low	High	Low	High	Low	High
2008	316.47	652.58	629.89	133	225	171	278	84	143	0.0%	0.1%	0.0%	0.0%	0.0%	0.0%
2009	320.52	661.36	647.77	413	643	533	762	286	415	0.1%	0.2%	0.1%	0.1%	0.0%	0.1%
2010	324.57	670.14	665.64	296	410	403	534	227	301	0.1%	0.1%	0.1%	0.1%	0.0%	0.0%
2011	328.62	678.91	683.52	281	443	383	542	222	307	0.1%	0.1%	0.1%	0.1%	0.0%	0.0%
2012	332.67	687.68	701.38	330	618	433	784	241	446	0.1%	0.2%	0.1%	0.1%	0.0%	0.1%
2013	336.72	696.45	719.26	228	370	252	408	113	191	0.1%	0.1%	0.0%	0.1%	0.0%	0.0%
2014	340.77	705.22	737.14	267	593	285	684	128	356	0.1%	0.2%	0.0%	0.1%	0.0%	0.0%
2015	344.81	713.98	755.00	270	455	286	483	129	228	0.1%	0.1%	0.0%	0.1%	0.0%	0.0%
2016	348.87	722.74	772.87	193	447	192	507	84	268	0.1%	0.1%	0.0%	0.1%	0.0%	0.0%
2017	352.97	731.61	791.17	171	253	168	251	75	114	0.0%	0.1%	0.0%	0.0%	0.0%	0.0%
2018	357.12	740.58	809.90	161	233	157	228	72	103	0.0%	0.1%	0.0%	0.0%	0.0%	0.0%
2019	361.31	749.67	829.07	158	240	153	233	71	107	0.0%	0.1%	0.0%	0.0%	0.0%	0.0%
2020	365.08	757.78	844.36	166	264	159	253	74	118	0.0%	0.1%	0.0%	0.0%	0.0%	0.0%
2021	369.13	766.54	862.23	317	516	372	565	209	307	0.1%	0.1%	0.0%	0.1%	0.0%	0.0%
2022	373.23	775.39	880.48	194	531	183	576	86	314	0.1%	0.1%	0.0%	0.1%	0.0%	0.0%
2023	377.37	784.35	899.11	201	308	187	286	89	139	0.1%	0.1%	0.0%	0.0%	0.0%	0.0%
2024	381.56	793.41	918.14	204	315	188	288	91	142	0.1%	0.1%	0.0%	0.0%	0.0%	0.0%
2025	385.34	801.55	933.71	203	313	184	281	90	139	0.1%	0.1%	0.0%	0.0%	0.0%	0.0%
2026	389.39	810.30	951.57	203	316	182	280	91	141	0.1%	0.1%	0.0%	0.0%	0.0%	0.0%
2027	393.49	819.14	969.78	204	324	180	283	90	145	0.1%	0.1%	0.0%	0.0%	0.0%	0.0%
2028	397.63	828.07	988.33	208	330	181	284	93	148	0.1%	0.1%	0.0%	0.0%	0.0%	0.0%
2029	401.82	837.10	1,007.24	211	333	181	284	94	149	0.1%	0.1%	0.0%	0.0%	0.0%	0.0%
2030	405.61	845.27	1,023.03	211	334	180	282	95	150	0.1%	0.1%	0.0%	0.0%	0.0%	0.0%
2031	409.88	854.49	1,042.60	212	331	179	277	95	149	0.1%	0.1%	0.0%	0.0%	0.0%	0.0%
2032	414.19	863.81	1,062.55	209	327	175	272	94	148	0.1%	0.1%	0.0%	0.0%	0.0%	0.0%
2033	418.55	873.24	1,082.88	205	319	171	264	92	144	0.0%	0.1%	0.0%	0.0%	0.0%	0.0%
2034	422.95	882.76	1,103.60	200	310	166	256	90	140	0.0%	0.1%	0.0%	0.0%	0.0%	0.0%
2035	427.40	892.39	1,124.71	193	296	159	244	87	134	0.0%	0.1%	0.0%	0.0%	0.0%	0.0%
2036	431.90	902.12	1,146.23	183	279	151	229	82	126	0.0%	0.1%	0.0%	0.0%	0.0%	0.0%
2037	436.45	911.97	1,168.16	172	259	142	213	77	117	0.0%	0.1%	0.0%	0.0%	0.0%	0.0%
2038	441.04	921.91	1,190.51	163	244	136	202	76	113	0.0%	0.1%	0.0%	0.0%	0.0%	0.0%
2039	445.68	931.97	1,213.29	184	262	168	232	101	138	0.0%	0.1%	0.0%	0.0%	0.0%	0.0%
2040	450.37	942.14	1,236.50	155	225	138	196	78	111	0.0%	0.1%	0.0%	0.0%	0.0%	0.0%
2041	455.11	952.41	1,260.16	149	233	135	211	78	122	0.0%	0.1%	0.0%	0.0%	0.0%	0.0%
2042	459.89	962.80	1,284.27	119	199	99	166	54	95	0.0%	0.0%	0.0%	0.0%	0.0%	0.0%
2043	464.73	973.31	1,308.84	112	206	94	180	52	107	0.0%	0.0%	0.0%	0.0%	0.0%	0.0%
2044	469.62	983.92	1,333.88	107	182	90	154	50	92	0.0%	0.0%	0.0%	0.0%	0.0%	0.0%
2045	474.56	994.66	1,359.40	100	183	84	162	47	97	0.0%	0.0%	0.0%	0.0%	0.0%	0.0%
2046	479.56	1,005.51	1,385.41	92	156	77	131	43	77	0.0%	0.0%	0.0%	0.0%	0.0%	0.0%
2047	484.60	1,016.47	1,411.92	85	146	71	123	39	71	0.0%	0.0%	0.0%	0.0%	0.0%	0.0%

* Direct, indirect, and induced.
[1] Source: Woods & Poole Economics, Inc., 2007.
[2] Source: Table 4-23 of the Multisale EIS.

Additional supplemental information is available regarding current economic conditions in the GOM region, particularly as it relates the recovery to date from the 2005 hurricanes. However, this new information (summarized below) does not in any way change the baseline population and employment projections used to analyze impacts of a typical WPA sale and the OCS Program, the methodologies used, or the conclusions presented in the Multisale EIS.

Two years after Hurricanes Katrina and Rita the recovery remains uneven throughout the areas originally affected. Areas where the most severe problems remain are Orleans and St. Bernard Parishes, Louisiana, and Hancock County, Mississippi. Affordable housing continues to be a problem in these areas, particularly in New Orleans. Adding to the problem is the high cost of insurance and building materials, causing many prospective developers to postpone projects until these pressures ease somewhat. Recovery is well underway in Jefferson and Calcasieu Parishes, Louisiana, as well as in Biloxi, Gulfport, and Pascagoula, Mississippi; and Bayou La Batre, Alabama. Recovery is driving expansion in East Baton Rouge and St. Tammany Parishes in Louisiana; Jackson, Hattiesburg, and Laurel, Mississippi; and in Gulf Shores and Mobile, Alabama. The measures of recovery are the functions of local government, population, crime, economic and fiscal effects, local government budgets, housing, and labor (Rowley, 2007).

Researchers continue to study the employment impacts of the 2005 hurricane season. The Bureau of Labor Statistics did a special review of the employment impacts of Hurricane Katrina and found that St. Bernard, Orleans, and Jefferson Parishes had the largest percent declines in employment between September 2004 and September 2006 (38%, 27%, and 24.5%, respectively). In the two months following Hurricane Katrina, nonfarm payroll employment in Louisiana fell by 241,000, a decline of 12 percent; in the New Orleans metro area, employment declined by 215,000, or 35 percent. In the New Orleans metro area in June 2006, it was 30 percent below the level a year earlier. Total nonfarm employment in Louisiana decreased by 184,600 jobs or 9.6 percent from September 2004 to September 2005, and in May 2006, the year-to-year loss was 177,700 jobs or 9.1 percent (U.S. Dept. of Labor, Bureau of Labor Statistics, 2006; pages 2, 4, 6, 8, 27, and 28). More recent data, however, show nonfarm payroll employment in Louisiana increasing 3.8 percent between April 2006 and April 2007 (one of the largest over-the-year percentage gains in employment for a State), or an increase of 69,500 from 1,835,700 to 1,905,200 (U.S. Dept. of Labor, Bureau of Labor Statistics, 2007).

Estimating employment data has proven more difficult post-Katrina, and some previous estimates are being revised as data-gathering limitations are addressed. For example, the Atlanta Federal Reserve Bank announced a revision to their employment estimates for Louisiana from 1,766,400 to 1,844,300 (an increase of 77,900 or 4.4%) between March 2005 and March 2006. Much of the revision was to account for job growth in the State's construction industry that had been underestimated due to survey sampling issues (such as identifying and sampling new construction businesses). Professional and business services is another industry where employment in Louisiana appears to have been originally underestimated (Federal Reserve Bank of Atlanta, 2006).

Researchers also continue to examine the impacts of the 2005 hurricane season on businesses in the region. For example, a Louisiana State University report on the hurricanes' effect on businesses comparing the second quarter of 2005 with the second quarter of 2006 concludes that, after a decline of over 5,000 in the number of employers (5.3%), the entire State of Louisiana had 2,270 fewer employers (2.3%) one year after the hurricanes (Terrell and Bilbo, 2007). The business failure rate in the year after the storms was 11.7 percent for the State as a whole compared with 26.5 percent for the five parish Southeast region.

The MMS has reexamined the analysis for economic factors presented in the Multisale EIS, based on the additional information presented above. No new significant information was discovered that would alter the impact conclusion for economic factors presented in the Multisale EIS; therefore, a complete new analysis of the potential impacts of proposed Lease Sale 207 on economic factors is not required. The analysis and potential impacts detailed in the Multisale EIS still apply for proposed Lease Sale 207.

4.2.13.4. Environmental Justice

The description of the environment for environmental justice can be found in Chapter 3.3.5.10 of the Multisale EIS. Detailed analysis of the routine, accidental, and cumulative impacts of proposed Lease Sale 207 on environmental justice can be found in Chapters 4.2.1.15.4, 4.4.14.4, and 4.5.15.4, respectively. The following is a summary of the impact analysis from the Multisale EIS.

Because of the presence of an extensive and widespread support system for OCS and associated labor force, the effects of proposed Lease Sale 207 are expected to be widely distributed and, except in Louisiana, little felt. In general, the infrastructural needs generated by proposed Lease Sale 207 will be met by the existing support systems, and these effects will be negligible. In general, who will be hired and where new infrastructure might be located is impossible to predict. A new C-Port (multiservices port terminal facility) in Galveston may be developed and this would likely increase Texas' share of the effects. However, this would occur in an already highly industrialized area so its effects would be primarily economic. For these reasons, impacts related to proposed Lease Sale 207 are expected to be economic and have a limited but positive effect on low-income and minority populations. Given the existing distribution of the industry and the limited concentrations of minority and low-income people, proposed Lease Sale 207 is not expected to have a disproportionate effect on these populations.

Lafourche Parish, Louisiana, will experience the most concentrated effects of proposed Lease Sale 207; however, because the parish is not heavily low-income or minority and because the effects of road traffic and port expansion will not occur in areas of low-income or minority concentration, these groups are not expected to be affected differentially.

Proposed Lease Sale 207 would help to maintain ongoing levels of activity rather than expand them. Future changes in activity levels will most likely be caused by fluctuations in oil prices and imports, and not be activities related to proposed Lease Sale 207. Routine impacts associated with proposed Lease Sale 207 are not expected to have disproportionate high/adverse environmental or health effects on minority or low-income populations.

With respect to accidental events, considering the low likelihood of an oil spill and the heterogeneous population distribution along the GOM region, accidental spill events associated with proposed Lease Sale 207 are not expected to have disproportionate adverse environmental or health effects on minority or low-income people.

In the GOM coastal area, the contribution of proposed Lease Sale 207 and the OCS Program to the cumulative effects of all activities and trends affecting environmental justice issues over the next 40 years is expected to be negligible to minor. The cumulative effects will be concentrated in coastal areas, and particularly, Louisiana. Most OCS Program effects are expected to be in the areas of job creation and the stimulation of the economy and are expected to make a small yet positive contribution to an area's economy. The contribution of the cumulative OCS Program to the cumulative impacts of all factors affecting environmental justice is expected to be minor (USDOI, MMS, 2001); therefore, the incremental contribution of proposed Lease Sale 207 to the cumulative impacts would also be minor.

A search was conducted for new information published since completion of the Multisale EIS. Analysis of FEMA storm damage data shows that Hurricane Katrina's impact was disproportionately borne by the region's African American community, by people who rented their homes, and by the poor and unemployed. More than one-third of the region's 1.7 million residents lived in areas that suffered flooding or moderate to catastrophic storm damage, according to FEMA. The majority of people living in damaged areas were in the City of New Orleans (over 350,000), with additional concentrations in suburban Jefferson Parish (175,000) and St. Bernard Parish (53,000) and along the Mississippi Coast (54,000). In the region as a whole, the disparities in storm damage are shown in the following comparisons (arranged in order of the degree of disparity): by race—damaged areas were 46 percent black, compared with 26 percent in undamaged areas; by housing tenure—46 percent of homes in damaged areas were occupied by renters, compared with 31 percent in undamaged communities; and by poverty and employment status—21 percent of households had incomes below the poverty line in damaged areas, compared with 15 percent in undamaged areas, and 7.6 percent of persons in the labor force were unemployed in damaged areas (before the storm), compared to 6.0 percent in undamaged areas. These comparisons are heavily influenced by the experience of the City of New Orleans. Outside the city, there were actually smaller shares of African American, poor, and unemployed residents in the damaged areas. Closer inspection of neighborhoods within New Orleans shows that some affluent white neighborhoods were hard hit, while some poor minority neighborhoods were spared. Yet, if the post-Katrina city were limited to the population previously living in areas that were undamaged by the storm— that is, if people were unable or unwilling to return to destroyed and damaged neighborhoods—New Orleans is at risk of losing more than 80 percent of its black population (Logan, 2007).

The Multisale EIS states the following: "Evidence also suggests that a healthy offshore petroleum industry also indirectly benefits low-income and minority populations." One MMS study in Louisiana found income inequality decreased during the oil boom and increased with the decline (Tolbert, 1995). The following updated information relates to this point.

A follow-up study to Tolbert (1995) about Abbeville, Louisiana, resulted in the following findings. A study component of a plant closure in Abbeville found that more employment opportunities exist within the community and surrounding area because, indirectly, growth of the oil and gas industry has served as an impetus in creating other labor market opportunities. A study component of industrial composition finds that a key source of sustainability from economic fluctuations at one time may be problematic at another time. Conversely, a problematic sector of the local economy at one time period may be proven to be a stabilizing sector at another time. These sectors include the oil and gas industry, manufacturing, and others. The particular lesson in the Abbeville context is that shifting sectors can be sustained by strong business services and professional sectors. Industrial diversity in Abbeville is dynamic overtime. The conclusions of Tolbert (2006) appear to qualify the conclusions of Tolbert (1995).

The MMS has reexamined the analysis for environmental justice presented in the Multisale EIS, based on the additional information presented above. No new significant information was discovered that would alter the impact conclusion for environmental justice presented in the Multisale EIS; therefore, a new analysis of the potential impacts of proposed Lease Sale 207 on environmental justice is not required. The analysis and potential impacts detailed in the Multisale EIS still apply for proposed Lease Sale 207.

5.   CONSULTATION AND COORDINATION

5.1.   SCOPING AND ACTIVITIES IN SUPPORT OF THE ENVIRONMENTAL ASSESSMENT FOR THE WESTERN PLANNING AREA'S PROPOSED LEASE SALE 207

The MMS performs ongoing external and internal scoping in order to determine the breadth and depth necessary for environmental analysis.

External Scoping: The scoping process for this EA was formally initiated on December 3, 2007, with the *Federal Register* notice announcing the preparation of an EA. In the notice, MMS requested that interested parties submit comments regarding any new information or issues that should be addressed in the EA. The comment period closed on January 3, 2008. Scoping and coordination efforts continue throughout the lease sale process and have been conducted since the publication of the Multisale EIS in 2007:

- On March 1, 2007, in Pensacola, Florida, and March 7, 2007, in Larose, Louisiana, to solicit comments regarding new information or issues that should be addressed in the Draft Supplemental EIS (SEIS) for EPA Lease Sale 224 held in March 2008.

- Scoping meetings were held on October 9, 2007 in Larose, Louisiana, October 10, in Baton Rouge, Louisiana, October 11, in Mobile, Alabama, and October 11, in Houston, Texas, to solicit comments regarding new information or issues that should be addressed in the Draft Supplemental EIS (SEIS) for CPA Lease Sale 208 in the area referred to as the "181 South Area." to be held in March 2009.

- Before a decision is made on the Final Notice of Sale, MMS will send the Consistency Determinations (CD) for WPA Lease Sale 207 to the States of Texas and Louisiana, documenting the consistency of the proposed sale with the coastal zone management (CZM) program. The States' comments on the Lease Sale 207 CD's are due within 60-days. If no comments are provided, MMS presumes the State's concurrence with the CD pursuant to the provisions of regulations at 15 CFR 930.41(a). If comments are provided, MMS will respond to them.

- On December 3, 2007, MMS published a Notice of Preparation of an EA on proposed Lease Sale 207. In the notice, MMS requested interested parties to submit comments regarding any new information or issues that should be addressed in the EA within 30 days. MMS received comments from the State of Louisiana Governor's Office on December 26, 2007 that are discussed below.

Internal Scoping: Internal scoping is an ongoing activity for all environmental projects and NEPA documents. Part of internal scoping involves reviewing resource estimates and oil-spill modeling results used in the preparation of the Multisale EIS to determine if they are still valid. The MMS GOM Region's Office of Resource Evaluation reviewed the oil and gas resource projections and associated activities for WPA Lease Sale 207 and confirmed that they remain within the range of those projected by MMS for a "typical WPA lease sale." The MMS Headquarters' Oil-Spill Risk Analysis (OSRA) group confirmed that results from the OSRA model summarized in the Multisale EIS and presented in a separate MMS report (USDOI, MMS, 2007i) are still valid for the proposed lease sale.

Internal scoping also requires MMS subject matter experts and analysts and NEPA coordinators to continuously update their knowledge base and incorporate three primary informational components into their analyses:

(1) recent studies/reports;

(2) monitoring results; and

(3) related cumulative-impact data.

The MMS's resource analysts and NEPA coordinators take an active role in the preparation, execution, and peer review of studies and reports developed under MMS's Environmental Studies Program. Some MMS analysts are involved in studies within their areas of expertise, as well as managing contracts for work conducted by other Federal/State agencies and universities conducting research in support of GOM's mission. The MMS staff participates in protected species observation cruises, and a dive team examines the marine biological activity around OCS infrastructure and investigates archaeological sites. The information obtained from these studies, as well as other relevant, non-MMS research, was considered by each subject matter expert in their assessment for this EA. Appendix C of the Multisale EIS lists the GOM Region's studies published from 2003 to 2006. Technical summaries for MMS-sponsored studies are available on our Internet website (http://www.gomr.mms.gov/homepg/regulate/environ/techsumm/rec_pubs.html).

Cumulative analyses are prepared by MMS subject matter experts that consider activities that could occur and may adversely affect GOM resources, including proposed WPA Lease Sale 207, prior and future OCS lease sales, State oil and gas activities, and other governmental and private projects and activities. The MMS analysts are often responsible for reviewing GOM activities not associated with oil and gas operations. All information gained from cumulative analyses was considered by MMS analysts in their assessments for this EA.

5.2. CONSULTATION AND COORDINATION CALENDAR

A complete description of all consultation and coordination activities and meetings is included in Chapter 5 of the Multisale EIS. A brief summary of these events follows:

Multisale EIS Process	
March 7, 2006	The Notice of Intent (NOI) for the proposed 2007-2012 CPA and WPA lease sales was published in the *Federal Register*. A 45-day comment period was provided; it closed on April 21, 2006. Additional public notices were distributed via newspaper notices, mailed notices, and the Internet. The MMS received 65 scoping letters in response to the NOI, which are summarized in Chapter 5.3.1 of the Multisale EIS.
March 28-30, 2006 *April 6, 2006*	The MMS held scoping meetings in Houston, Texas; Harahan, Louisiana; Mobile, Alabama; and Tallahassee, Florida, to receive comments on the Draft EIS for the proposed 2007-2012 CPA and WPA lease sales. A summary of comments presented at the scoping meetings is provided in Chapter 5.3.1 of the Multisale EIS.
April 28, 2006	The Call for Information and Nominations (Call) for the proposed 2007-2012 lease sales was published in the *Federal Register*. A 30-day comment period was provided; it closed on May 30, 2006. The MMS received five comment letters in response to the Call, which are summarized in Chapter 5.3.3 of the Multisale EIS.
December 5-7, 2006	The MMS held public hearings in Houston, Texas; New Orleans and Larose, Louisiana; Panama City, Florida; and Mobile, Alabama, to receive comments on the Draft Multisale EIS for CPA Lease Sales 205, 206, 208, 213, 216, and 222, and WPA Lease Sales 204, 207, 210, 215, and 218. There were no speakers at the Houston, Mobile, and Larose hearings. One individual presented comments at the New Orleans hearing and 26 at the Larose hearing. The comments are summarized in Chapter 5.5 of the Multisale EIS.
December 12, 2006	The EFH programmatic consultation was initiated and completed for the 2007-2012 lease sales, including Lease Sale 207. The NMFS concurred by letter dated December 12, 2006, that the information presented in the Draft Multisale EIS satisfies the EFH consultation procedures outlined in 50 CFR

	600.920, and as specified in our March 17, 2000, findings. Provided MMS proposed mitigations, previous EFH conservation recommendations, and the standard lease stipulations and regulations are followed as proposed, NMFS agrees that impacts on EFH and associated fishery resources resulting from activities conducted under the 2007-2012 lease sales would be minimal. Therefore, unless future changes to the proposed 2007-2012 lease sales are proposed or new information becomes available, no further EFH consultation is required for the 2007-2012 lease sales.
June 28, 2007	The FWS and MMS have consulted informally per FWS guidance. A draft copy of the Biological Assessment, prepared by MMS, was submitted as requested by FWS (USDOI, MMS, 2007j). On June 28, 2007, MMS received oral confirmation from FWS that the consultation will remain informal; therefore there will be no new mitigations or Terms and Conditions from FWS. The final Biological Assessment and a request for a Letter of Concurrence were submitted to FWS on August 3, 2007. The FWS submitted a Letter of Concurrence dated September 14, 2007.
June 29, 2007	The NMFS BO was signed on June 29, 2007, and has been received by MMS. The BO concludes that the proposed lease sales and associated activities in the GOM in the 2007-2012 OCS Leasing Program, including Lease Sale 207, are not likely to jeopardize the continued existence of threatened and endangered species under NMFS jurisdiction, or destroy or adversely modify designated critical habitat. The NMFS issued an Incidental Take Statement on sea turtle species, which contains reasonable and prudent measures with implementing terms and conditions to help minimize take.

WPA Lease Sale 207 EA Process

December 3, 2007	The MMS published a Notice of Preparation of an EA on proposed WPA Lease Sale 207. In the notice, MMS requested interested parties to submit comments within 30 days regarding any new information or issues that should be addressed in the EA.
December 26, 2007	The State of Louisiana Governor's Office provided general comments on preparation of the EA in a 3-page letter. Four concerns were expressed.
	(1) The MMS is relying on an outdated environmental baseline and has yet to document a full assessment of the increased risk faced by Louisiana from global warming and related future increases in sea level rise and hurricane intensity.
	(2) The MMS uses estimates, assumptions, and projections of anticipated wetland losses and other types of impacts to Louisiana resulting from lease sale programs, but has yet to validate or verify those estimates, assumptions, and projections with after-sale analyses to refine or replace the predictive techniques that were used.
	(3) The MMS has yet to take responsibility or propose mitigation for the OCS-related activities that contribute to direct, indirect, and cumulative impacts on wetlands, but also the "incremental impact of the action when added to other past, present, and reasonably foreseeable future actions."
	(4) The MMS should describe improvements on survivability of facilities and OCS infrastructure, such as platforms and pipelines, that better able them to withstand the high sea states from storm activity in the Gulf of Mexico. The EA should assess the impacts of storm-generated debris from OCS structures on other users of the OCS.

6. REFERENCES CITED

Ache, B. 2007. Written communication. National Oceanic and Atmospheric Administration. Email to the Gulf of Mexico Alliance Water Quality Team. Various emails sent in June 2007 in preparation for the annual July 2007 meeting.

American Gaming Association (AGA). 2003. State of the states: The AGA survey of casino entertainment. 32 pp. Internet website: http://www.americangaming.org/assets/files/AGA_survey_2003.pdf. Accessed July 9, 2007.

American Gaming Association (AGA). 2007. State of the states: The AGA survey of casino entertainment. Internet website: http://www.americangaming.org/survey/index.cfm. Accessed August 13, 2007.

American Petroleum Institute (API). 2006. Bulletin 2TD, Guidelines for tie-downs on offshore production facilities for the hurricane season, first edition. Internet website: http://www.api.org/Publications/2005-hurricane.cfm.

American Petroleum Institute (API). 2007. Gulf of Mexico MODU mooring practices for the 2007 hurricane season—interim recommendations. API Recommended Practice 95F, second edition, April 2007. Internet website: http://api-ec.api.org/Publications/upload/95F_2-3.pdf. 52 pp.

Ashton, P.K., R.A. Speir, and L.O. Upton III. 2004. Modeling exploration, development, and production in the Gulf of Mexico. Volumes I-III. U.S. Dept. of the Interior, Minerals Management Service, Environmental Studies Program, Herndon, VA. OCS Study MMS 2004-018.

Associated Press. 2007. Floods bring 'dead zone' to Texas gulf, expert says: Sea life is threatened, but loss is expected to be temporary. *St. Petersburg Times*. Internet website. http://tampabay.com/2007/08/01/Worldandnation/Floods_bring_dead_zo.shtml. Posted August 1, 2007. Accessed December 5, 2007.

Balseiro, A., A. Espi, I. Marquez, V. Perez, M.C. Ferreras, J.F. Garcia Marin, and J.M. Prieto. 2005. Pathological features in marine birds affected by the *Prestige*'s oil spill in the north of Spain. Journal of Wildlife Diseases 41:371-378.

Barcott, B. 2007. Kill the cat that kills the bird? *New York Times*, New York, NY. December 2, 2007. Internet website: http://www.nytimes.com/2007/12/02/magazine/02cats-v--birds-t.html.

Barras, J.A., S. Beville, D. Britsch, S. Hartley, S. Hawes, J. Johnston, P. Kemp, Q. Kinler, A. Martucci, J. Porthouse, D. Reed, K. Roy, S. Sapkota, and J. Suhayda. 2003. Historical and projected coastal Louisiana land changes: 1978-2050. USGS Open File Report 03-334.

Barras, J.A. 2006. Land area change in coastal Louisiana after the 2005 hurricanes: A series of three maps. USGS Open File Report 06-1274. U.S. Dept. of the Interior, Geological Survey.

Barras, J.A. 2007. Personal communication. Status of any further analysis of post-Katrina barrier island or mainland beach damages in Louisiana, Alabama, and Mississippi coasts. U.S. Dept. of the Interior, Geological Survey, National Wetlands Research Center, Lafayette, LA.

Barras, J.A. 2007. Satellite images and aerial photographs of the effects of Hurricanes Katrina and Rita on coastal Louisiana: USGS Data Series 281. Internet website: http://pubs.usgs.gov/ds/2007/281.

Barras, J.A. In press. Land area changes in coastal Louisiana after Hurricanes Katrina and Rita. In: Farris, G.S., G.J. Smith, M.P. Crane, C.R. Demas, L.L. Robbins, and D.L. Lavoie, eds. Science and the storms—The USGS response to the hurricanes of 2005. U.S. Dept. of the Interior, Geological Survey. Geological Survey Circular 1306. Internet website: http://pubs.usgs.gov/ds/2007/281/intro.htm.

Bass, A.S. and R.E. Turner. 1997. Relationships between salt marsh loss and dredge canals in three Louisiana estuaries. Journal of Coastal Research 13(3):895-903.

Bernier, J.C., R.A. Morton, and J.A. Barras. 2006. Constraining rates and trends of historical wetland loss, Mississippi River Delta Plain, south-central Louisiana. Coastal Environment and Water Quality, Water Resources Publications, LLC, Highlands Ranch, CO. Pp. 371-382. Internet website: http://coastal.er.usgs.gov/gc-subsidence/historical-wetland-loss.html.

Boesch, D.F., A. Mehta, J. Morris, W. Nuttle, C. Simenstad, and D. Swift. 1994. Scientific assessment of coastal wetland loss, restoration and management in Louisiana. Journal of Coastal Research 20:1-103.

Bowles, A. 2007. Personal communication. Senior Research Biologist, Hubb-Sea World Research Institute, San Diego, CA. June 1, 2007.

Britsch, L.D. and J.B. Dunbar. 1993. Land-loss rates Louisiana coastal plain. Journal of Coastal Research 9:324-338.

Burger, A.E. 1993. Estimating the mortality of seabirds following oil spills: Effects of spill volume. Marine Pollution 26:140-143.

Burger, J. 1997. Oil spills. New Brunswick, NJ: Rutgers University Press. 261 pp.

Cahoon, D.R. Personal communication. 2007. Verification of pipeline and navigation canal erosion rates. U.S. Dept of the Interior, Geological Survey, Patuxent Wildlife Research Center. July 2007.

Church, R., D. Warren, R. Cullimore, L. Johnston, W. Schroeder, W. Patterson, T. Shirley. M. Kilgour, N. Morris, and J. Moore. 2007. Archaeological and biological analysis of World War II shipwrecks in the Gulf of Mexico: Artificial reef effect in deep water. U.S. Dept. of the Interior, Minerals Management Service, Gulf of Mexico OCS Region, New Orleans, LA. OCS Study MMS 2007-015. 387 pp.

Clark, R. 2007. Personal communication. Status of additional information or studies concerning post-Katrina storm damage to barrier islands and mainland beaches. Florida Dept. of Environmental Protection, Bureau of Beaches and Coastal Systems. May 2007.

Clark, R.R. and J.W. LaGrone. 2006. Hurricane Dennis & Hurricane Katrina: Final report on 2005 hurricane season impacts on northwest Florida. Florida Dept. of Environmental Protection, Division of Water Resource Management, Bureau of Beaches and Coastal Systems. 122 pp. Internet website: http://bcs.dep.state.fl.us/reports/2005/2005hurr.pdf. Accessed June 26, 2007.

Continental Shelf Associates, Inc. (CSA). 2007. Characterization of northern Gulf of Mexico deepwater hard-bottom communities with emphasis on *Lophelia* coral. U.S. Dept. of the Interior, Minerals Management Service, Gulf of Mexico OCS Region, New Orleans, LA. OCS Study MMS 2007-044. 169 pp. + app.

Dismukes, D. 2007. Personal communication. Louisiana State University, Center for Energy Studies, Baton Rouge, LA.

Dismukes, D.E., M. Barnett, D. Vitrano, and K. Strellec. 2007. Gulf of Mexico OCS oil and gas scenario examination: Onshore waste disposal. U.S. Dept. of the Interior, Minerals Management Service, Gulf of Mexico OCS Region, New Orleans, LA. OCS Report MMS 2007-051. 5 pp.

Dokka, R.K., G.F. Sella, and T.H. Dixon. 2006. Tectonic control of subsidence and southward displacement of southeast Louisiana with respect to stable North America. American Geophysical Union. Geophysical Research Letters, Vol. 33. L23308. http://wwwest.ngs.noaa.gov/CORS/Articles/2006GL027250.pdf

Dokken, Q.R., I.R. MacDonald, J.W. Tunnell, Jr., T. Wade, K. Withers, S.J. Dilworth, T.W. Bates, C.R. Beaver, and C.M. Rinaud. 2003. Long-term monitoring of the East and West Flower Garden Banks National Marine Sanctuary, 1998-2001: Final report. U.S. Dept. of the Interior, Minerals Management Service, Gulf of Mexico OCS Region, New Orleans, LA. OCS Study MMS 2003-031. 89 pp.

Durako, M.J., M.O. Hall, F. Sargent, and S. Peck. 1992. Propeller scars in sea grass beds: an assessment and experimental study of recolonization in Weedon Island State Preserve, Florida. In: Web, F., ed. Proceedings, 19th Annual Conference of Wetland Restoration and Creation. Hillsborough Community College, Tampa, FL. Pp. 42-53.

Federal Reserve Bank of Atlanta. 2006. Econ South. Volume 8, Number 4, Fourth Quarter 2006. Southeastern economy to grow modestly in 2007: State profiles—Louisiana. Louisiana continues march toward recovery—Louisiana employment: Better than the data suggest. Internet website: http://www.frbatlanta.org. Accessed June 14, 2007.

Fisher, M. Personal communication. 2008. Recreational Fishing Statistics for Texas in 2006. Texas Parks and Wildlife Department, Rockport Laboratory, Rockport, TX.

Flint, B. 2007. Personal communication. Wildlife Biologist, Pacific Remote Islands National Wildlife Refuge Complex, U.S. Dept. of the Interior, Fish and Wildlife Service, Honolulu, HI. June 11, 2007.

Florida State Dept. of Environmental Protection (FDEP). Bureau of Beaches and Coastal Systems. 2005. About beach and coastal data. April 20, 2005. Internet website: http://www.dep.state.fl.us/beaches/data/data.htm

Florida State Dept. of Environmental Protection (FDEP). Bureau of Beaches and Coastal Systems. 2007. Beaches and coastal systems. August 31, 2007. Internet website: http://www.dep.state.fl.us/beaches/. Accessed June 28, 2007.

General Accountability Office. 2007. Coastal wetlands: Lessons learned from past efforts in Louisiana could help guide future restoration and protection. General Accountability Office, GAO 08-130. Washington DC. 57 pp. Internet website: http://www.gao.gov/new.items/d08130.pdf.

Geraci, J.R. and D.J. St. Aubin. 1980. Offshore petroleum resource development and marine mammals: A review and research recommendations. Marine Fisheries Review 42:1-12.

Geraci, J.R., and D.J. St. Aubin. 1987. Effects of offshore oil and gas development on marine mammals and turtles. In: Boesch, D.F. and N.N. Rabalais, eds. Long-term environmental effects of offshore oil and gas development. London: Elsevier Applied Science.

Google. 2007. Google advanced scholar search. Internet website: http://scholar.google.com/advanced_scholar_search?hl=en&h=&ie=UTF-8. Accessed June 11, 2007.

Haig, S.H. and C.L. Ferland. 2002. 2001 international piping plover census. U.S. Dept. of the Interior, Geological Survey, Forest and Rangeland Ecosystem Science Center, Corvallis, OR. 293 pp.

Hall, D. 2006. U.S. Dept. of the Interior, Fish and Wildlife Service. Congressional testimony, Hurricane Katrina damage to USFWS refuges. Internet website: http://www.fws.gov/laws/Testimony/109th/2006/Dale%20Hall%20Impact%20of%20Hurrican%20Katrina%20on%20NWR%20march%2016%202006.htm.

Haney, J.L., Y. Wei, and S.G. Douglas. In preparation. Synthesis and integration of meteorological/air quality data study. U.S. Dept. of the Interior, Minerals Management Service, Gulf of Mexico OCS Region, New Orleans, LA.

Hardegree, B. 2007. Texas seagrass: Status, statewide issues, and restoration. Gulf of Mexico Alliance Regional Restoration Coordination Team Workshop, Galveston, TX. Internet website: http://www2.nos.noaa.gov/gomex/restoration/workshops/workshops.html.

Hartung, R. 1995. Assessment of the potential for long-term toxicological effects of the *Exxon Valdez* oil spill on birds and mammals. In: Wells, P.G., J.N.; Butler, and J.S. Hughes, eds. *Exxon Valdez* oil spill: Fate and effects in Alaskan waters. American Society for Testing and Materials, Philadelphia, PA. ASTM STP 1219.

Iledare, O.O. and M.J. Kaiser. 2007. Competition and performance in oil and gas lease sales and development in the U.S. Gulf of Mexico OCS region, 1983-1999. U.S. Dept. of the Interior, Minerals

Management Service, Gulf of Mexico OCS Region, New Orleans, La. OCS Study MMS 2007-034. 106 pp.

Intergovernmental Panel on Climate Change. 2007. Climate Change 2007: Synthesis Report. Summary for Policymakers. Fourth Assessment Report, World Meteorological Organization and the United Nations Environment Programme, 24 pp. Internet website: http://www.ipcc.ch/pdf/assessment-report/ar4/syr/ar4_syr_spm.pdf.

Jankowski, M. 2007. Personal communication. Wildlife Disease Specialist, U.S. Dept. of the Interior, USGS/BRD, National Wildlife Health Center, Madison, WI. June 6, 2007.

Khan, R.A. and P. Ryan. 1991. Long-term effects of crude oil on common murres (*Uria aalge*) following rehabilitation. Bulletin of Environmental Contamination and Toxicology 46:216-222.

Kirkham, C. 2007. Storms muddy waters for La. fishers. *The Times-Picayune*, New Orleans, LA. May 20, 2007. Internet website: http://www.blog.nola.com/times-picayune/2007/05/storms_muddy_waters_for_la_fis.html.

Leadon, M.E. 2004. Hurricane Ivan: Beach and dune erosion and structural damage assessment and post-storm recovery plan for the Panhandle Coast of Florida. Florida Dept. of Environmental Protection, Division of Water Resources Management, Bureau of Beaches and Coastal Systems. 64 pp. Internet website: http://www.bcs.dep.state.fl.us/reports/ivan.pdf. Accessed June 28, 2007.

Leblanc, D. 2007. Personal communication. Biologist, U.S. Dept. of the Interior, Fish and Wildlife Service, Ecological Services, Daphne, AL. June 25, 2007.

Logan, J.R. 2007. The impact of Katrina: Race and class in storm-damaged neighborhoods. Brown University, Providence, RI. 16 pp. Internet website: http://www.s4.brown.edu/Katrina/report.pdf. Accessed July 10, 2007.

Louis Berger Group, Inc. 2004. OCS-related infrastructure in the Gulf of Mexico fact book. U.S. Dept. of the Interior, Minerals Management Service, Gulf of Mexico OCS Region, New Orleans, LA. OCS Study MMS 2004-027. 234 pp.

Louisiana Coastal Wetlands Conservation and Restoration Task Force. 1993. Coastal Wetland Planning, Protection, and Restoration Act: Louisiana coastal wetlands restoration plan; main report and environmental impact statement. Louisiana Coastal Wetlands Conservation and Restoration Task Force, Baton Rouge, LA.

Louisiana Dept. of Environmental Quality (LADEQ). 2007a. Water quality assessment in Louisiana. Internet website: http://www.deq.louisiana.gov/portal/Default.aspx?tabid=69. Accessed July 5, 2007.

Louisiana Dept. of Environmental Quality (LADEQ). 2007b. Beach sweep & inland waterway cleanup. Louisiana Dept. of Environmental Quality, Division of Environmental Assistance. Internet website: http://www.deq.louisiana.gov/portal/default.aspx?tabid=191. Accessed July 31, 2007.

Louisiana Dept. of Wildlife and Fisheries. 2005. LDWF advises boaters on Lake Pontchartrain and connecting waterways to remain alert for manatees in area. Louisiana Fisheries. Archived News 2005. Internet website. http://www.seagrantfish.lsu.edu/news/2005/manatee.htm. Posted August 1, 2005. Accessed December 4, 2007. 1 p.

Louisiana Dept. of Wildlife and Fisheries. 2007. Estimates indicate Katrina and Rita could cost the State's fisheries' industries $2.3 billion. Internet website: http://www.louisianaseafood.com/news.cfm?ArticleID=126. Accessed July 10, 2007.

Louisiana Universities Marine Consortium (LUMCON). 2007a. Hypoxia in the northern Gulf of Mexico. Internet website: http://www.gulfhypoxia.net/. Accessed July 5, 2007.

Louisiana Universities Marine Consortium (LUMCON). 2007b. Dead zone size near top end. Press Release, July 28, 2007. Internet website: http://www.gulfhypoxia.net/shelfwide07/PressRelease07.pdf. Accessed July 30, 2007.

May, C.A. 2007. Distribution, status, and trends of seagrasses in Mississippi. *Gulf of Mexico Alliance Regional Restoration Coordination Team Workshop*, March 6-9, 2007, Spanish Fort, AL. 15 pp. Internet website: http://www2.nos.noaa.gov/gomex/restoration/workshops/workshops.html.

Maze-Foley, K. and K. Mullin. 2006. Cetaceans of the oceanic northern Gulf of Mexico: Distributions, group sizes and interspecific associations. *Journal of Cetacean Research and Management* 8(2):203-213.

Mississippi Alabama Sea Grant Consortium. 2007. Mississippi coastal cleanup. Internet website: http://www.masgc.org/cleanup/index.htm. Accessed July 31, 2007.

Mississippi Gulf Coast Convention & Visitors Bureau. 2007. Gulf Coast gaming revenues. Internet website: http://www.gulfcoast.org/static/index.cfm?contentID=329. Accessed July 9, 2007.

Morton, B. 2007. Personal communication. Request for new post-Katrina storm damage information concerning Florida barrier islands and mainland beaches. U.S. Dept. of Interior, Geological Survey, Integrated Science Center, St. Petersburg, FL. May 2007.

Nicholls, J.L. and G.A. Baldassarre. 1990. Habitat associations of piping plovers wintering in the United States. *Wilson Bulletin* 102:581-590.

Nisbet, I.C.T. 2007. Personal communication. Chief, I.C.T. Nisbet & Co., North Falmouth, MA. June 4, 2007.

OCLC FirstSearch. 2007. Internet website: http://www.newfirstsearch.oclc.org/. Accessed June 11, 2007.

Palka, D. and M. Johnson, eds. 2007. Cooperative research to study dive patterns of sperm whales in the Atlantic Ocean. U.S. Dept. of the Interior, Minerals Management Service, Gulf of Mexico OCS Region, New Orleans, LA. OCS Study MMS 2007-033. 49 pp.

Parsons, K.C. 1994. The *Arthur Kill* oil spills: Biological effects in birds. In: Burger, J., ed. Before and after an oil spill: The *Arthur Kill*. New Brunswick, NJ: Rutgers University Press. Pp. 215-237.

PBS&J. In preparation. Impacts of recent hurricane activity on historic shipwrecks in the Gulf of Mexico. U.S. Dept. of the Interior, Minerals Management Service, Gulf of Mexico OCS Region, New Orleans, LA.

Penland, S., L. Wayne, L.D. Britsch, S.J. Williams, A.D. Beall, and V. Caridas Butterworth. 2001a. Geomorphic classification of coastal land loss between 1932 and 1990 in the Mississippi River Delta Plain, southeastern Louisiana. U.S. Dept. of the Interior, Geological Survey, Coastal and Marine Geology Program, Woods Hole Field Center, Woods Hole, MA. Open File Report 00-417.

Penland, S., L. Wayne, L.D. Britsch, S. J. Williams, A. D. Beall, and V. Caridas Butterworth. 2001b. Process classification of coastal land loss between 1932 and 1990 in the Mississippi River Delta Plain, southeastern Louisiana. U.S. Dept. of the Interior, Geological Survey, Coastal and Marine Geology Program, Woods Hole Field Center, Woods Hole, MA. Open File Report 00-418.

Pilkey, O.H. and K.L. Dixon. 1996. The corps and the shore. Washington, DC: Island Press. 272 pp.

Precht, W.F., R.B. Aronson, K.J.P. Deslarzes, M.L. Robbart, A. Gelber, and B. Zimmer. 2006. Long-term monitoring at the East and West Flower Garden Banks, 2002-2003: Final report. U.S. Dept. of the Interior, Minerals Management Service, Gulf of Mexico OCS Region, New Orleans, LA. OCS Study MMS 2006-035. 182 pp.

Precht, W.F., R.B. Aronson, K.J.P. Deslarzes, M.L. Robbart, A. Gelber., and B. Gearheart. In preparation (a). Post-hurricane assessment of sensitive habitats of the Flower Garden Banks vicinity: Draft report. U.S. Dept. of the Interior, Minerals Management Service, Gulf of Mexico OCS Region, New Orleans, LA.

Precht, W.F., R.B. Aronson, K.J.P. Deslarzes, M.L. Robbart, A. Gelber, and B. Zimmer. In preparation (b). Long-term monitoring at the East and West Flower Garden Banks, 2004: Final report. U.S. Dept. of the Interior, Minerals Management Service, Gulf of Mexico OCS Region, New Orleans, LA.

Rabalais, N.N., R.E. Turner, and D. Scavia. 2002. Beyond science into policy: Gulf of Mexico hypoxia and the Mississippi River. BioScience 52:129-142.

Rice, S.D., J.F. Karinen, and C.C. Brodersen. 1983. Effects of oiled sediment on juvenile king crab. U.S. Dept. of Commerce, National Oceanic and Atmospheric Administration, National Marine Fisheries Service, Northwest and Alaska Fisheries Center, Auke Bay Laboratory, Auke Bay, AK. Internet website: http://www.gomr.mms.gov/PI/PDFImages/ESPIS/0/976.pdf.

Rooker, J.R., R.T. Kraus, and R.L. Hill. In preparation. Spatial and temporal patterns of recruitment to mid- and outer-shelf banks in the NW Gulf of Mexico. Unpublished preliminary report. Texas A&M University, College Station, TX.

Rowley K. 2007. GulfGov reports: A year and a half after Katrina and Rita, an uneven recovery. Nelson A. Rockefeller Institute of Government, Albany, NY, and Public Affairs Research Council of Louisiana, Baton Rouge, LA. 73 pp. Internet website: http://www.rockinst.org/WorkArea/showcontent.aspx?id=9920.

Sargent, F.J., T.J. Leary, D.W. Crewz, and C.R. Kruer. 1995. Scarring of Florida's seagrasses: Assessment and management options. FRMI TR-1, Florida Marine Research Institute, St. Petersburg, FL. 37 pp. + app.

Scaife, W.B., R.E. Turner, and R. Costanza. 1983. Recent land loss and canal impacts in coastal Louisiana. Environmental Management 7:433-442.

Shigenaka, G. 2001. Toxicity of oil to reef-building corals: A spill response perspective. U.S. Dept. of Commerce, National Oceanic and Atmospheric Administration, Seattle, WA. NOAA Technical Memorandum NOS OR&R 8. 95 pp. Internet website: http://www.archive.orr.noaa.gov/oilaids/coral/pdfs/coral_tox.pdf.

Smith, R. 2007. Personal communication. 2006 international bird census. U.S. Dept. of the Interior, Fish and Wildlife Service, Ecological Services Office, Lafayette, LA.

Smultea, M. and B. Würsig. 1995. Bottlenose dolphin reactions to the *Mega Borg* oil spill. Aquatic Mammals 21:171-181.

Spalding, E.A. and M.W. Hester. 2007. Interactive effects of hydrology and salinity on oligohaline plant species productivity: Implications of relative sea-level rise. Estuaries and Coasts 30(2):214-225. Internet website: http://www.erf.org/cesn/vol30n2r4.html.

State of Louisiana. Coastal Protection and Restoration Authority (CPRA). 2007. Integrated ecosystem restoration and hurricane protection: Louisiana's comprehensive master plan for a sustainable coast. 140 pp. Internet website: http://www.lacpra.org/assets/docs/cprafinalreport_pg77_pg85_5-2-07.pdf.

Systems Applications International, Sonoma Technology, Inc., Earth Tech, Alpine Geophysics, and A.T. Kearney. 1995. Gulf of Mexico air quality study: Final report. Volumes I-III. U.S. Dept. of the Interior, Minerals Management Service, Gulf of Mexico OCS Region, New Orleans, LA. OCS Study MMS 95-0038, 95-0039, and 95-0040. 650, 214, and 190 pp., respectively.

Terrell, D. and R. Bilbo. 2007. A report on the impact of Hurricanes Katrina and Rita on Louisiana businesses: 2005Q2-2006Q2. Louisiana State University, Division of Economic Development, Baton Rouge, LA. 51 pp. Internet website: http://www.bus.lsu.edu/centers/ded/ or http://www.bus.lsu.edu/centers/ded/reports/2006Q4_Business_Report.pdf/.

Texas Commission on Environmental Quality. 2007. Texas Commission on Environmental Quality. Internet website: http://www.tceq.state.tx.us/. Accessed July 5, 2007.

Texas General Land Office (TGLO). 2007. Coastal Coordination Division. Internet website: Accessed July 9, 2007.

Texas Sea Grant. 2006. More Texas marinas participating in clean marina program. News Release, September 20, 2006. Internet website. http://www.texas-sea-grant.tamu.edu/pubs/press/cleanmarina.php. Accessed December 5, 2007.

Tolbert, C.M. 1995. Oil and gas development and coastal income inequality: A comparative analysis. U.S. Dept. of the Interior, Minerals Management Service, Gulf of Mexico OCS Region, New Orleans, LA.. OCS Study MMS 94-0052. 75 pp. [MMS updated certain information in this study: Tolbert, 2006.]

Tolbert, C.M. II, ed. 2006. Sustainable community in oil and gas country: Final report. U.S. Dept. of the Interior, Minerals Management Service, Gulf of Mexico OCS Region, New Orleans, LA.. OCS Study MMS 2006-011. 76 pp.

Travel Industry Association of America. 2003. 2002 TravelScope profile of U.S. travelers to Louisiana. The Research Department of the Travel Industry Association of America, Washington, DC. July 2003.

Travel Industry Association of America. 2004. 2003 TravelScope profile of U.S. travelers to Louisiana. The Research Department of the Travel Industry Association of America. Washington, DC. July 2004.

Travel Industry Association of America. 2005. 2004 TravelScope profile of U.S. travelers to Louisiana. The Research Department of the Travel Industry Association of America. Washington, DC. June 2005.

Tremplay, T. 2007. Personal communication. Request for current information concerning post-Katrina storm damage to Texas barrier islands and beaches. Texas Bureau of Economic Geology, Austin, TX. May 2007.

Turner, R.E., R. Costanza, and W. Scaife. 1982. Canals and wetland erosion rates in coastal Louisiana. In: Conference on Coastal Erosion and Wetland Modification in Louisiana: Causes, Consequences, and Options. U.S. Dept. of the Interior, Fish and Wildlife Service, Office of Biological Services. FWS/OBS 82/59.

Upton, L.O. III and P.K. Ashton. 2005. Measuring the impact of high oil prices and Federal policy initiatives in offshore Gulf of Mexico exploration, development, and production activity. Innovation & Information Consultants, Inc. Presentation, 25th Annual North American Conference of the United States Association for Energy Economics/International Association for Energy Economics, September 18-21, 2005, Denver CO. 16 pp. Internet website: http://www.iaee.org/documents/denver/upton.pdf.

U.S. Dept. of Commerce. Bureau of the Census. 2007. County business patterns. EPCD. Internet website: http://www.census.gov/epcd/cbp/view/cbpview.html. Accessed August 13-17, 2007.

U.S. Dept. of Commerce. National Marine Fisheries Service. 2005. National survey on recreation and the environment (NSRE). Internet website: http://www.marineeconomics.noaa.gov/NSRE/welcome.html. Accessed August 23, 2007.

U.S. Dept. of Commerce. National Marine Fisheries Service. 2007a. Endangered Species Act Section 7 consultation on the effects of the five-year outer continental shelf oil and gas leasing program (2007-2012) in the Central and Western Planning Areas of the Gulf of Mexico. Biological Opinion. June 29. F/SER/2006/02611. 127 pp.

U.S. Dept. of Commerce. National Marine Fisheries Service. 2007b. Report to Congress on the impact of Hurricanes Katrina, Rita, and Wilma on commercial and recreational fishery habitat of Alabama, Florida, Louisiana, Mississippi, and Texas. July 2007. 191 pp. + apps. Internet website: http://www.ecowatch.ncddc.noaa.gov/nmfs-report.

U.S. Dept. of Commerce. National Marine Fisheries Service. 2007c. Fish stock sustainability index (FSSI): Summary of stock status determination changes from April 1, 2007 through June 30, 2007. Status of U.S. fisheries, second quarter update, July 17, 2007. 2 pp. Internet website: http://www.nmfs.noaa.gov/sfa/domes_fish/StatusoFisheries/2007/SecondQuarter/Q2-2007-FSSISummaryChanges.pdf.

U.S. Dept. of Commerce. National Marine Fisheries Service. 2007d. Office of Science and Technology. Fisheries of the United States 2006 119 pp. Internet website: http://www.st.nmfs.gov/st1/fus/fus06/fus_2006.pdf. Accessed July 31, 2007.

U.S. Dept. of Commerce. National Marine Fisheries Service. 2007e. Marine recreational fisheries statistics survey, Gulf of Mexico. Internet website: http://www.st.nmfs.gov/st1/recreational/index.html. Accessed August 9, 2007.

U.S. Dept. of Commerce. National Marine Fisheries Service. 2007f. National survey on recreation and the environment (NSRE). Internet website: http://www.marineeconomics.noaa.gov/NSRE/. Accessed July 3, 2007.

U.S. Dept. of Commerce. National Oceanic and Atmospheric Administration. 2007. Gulf of Mexico Marine Debris Project. Internet website: http://www.gulfofmexico.marinedebris.noaa.gov/. Accessed July 11, 2007.

U.S. Dept. of Commerce. National Oceanic and Atmospheric Administration. Office of Response and Restoration. 2007. Summary points: 10 years of intertidal monitoring after the *Exxon Valdez* spill. Internet website: http://www.archive.orr.noaa.gov/bat/10years.html. Accessed September 11, 2007.

U.S. Dept. of Labor. Bureau of Labor Statistics. 2006. Review: Special issue, Hurricane Katrina. August 2006, Vol. 129, No. 8. 78 pp.

U.S. Dept. of Labor. Bureau of Labor Statistics. 2007. News. U.S. Dept. of Labor, Washington DC. USDL 07-0713. May 18, 2007.

U.S. Dept. of the Army. Corps of Engineers. 2004. Louisiana coastal area (LCA): Ecosystem restoration study. Volumes I and II. Draft programmatic environmental impact statement. U.S. Dept. of the Army, Corps of Engineers, New Orleans District, New Orleans, LA.

U.S. Dept. of the Interior, Fish and Wildlife Service and U.S. Dept. of Commerce, Bureau of the Census. 2001. National survey of fishing, hunting, and wildlife-associated recreation. U.S. Dept. of the Interior, Fish and Wildlife Service, Washington, DC. 170 pp.

U.S. Dept. of the Interior. Fish and Wildlife Service. 2007a. Bald eagle soars off endangered species list. News Release, June 28, 2007. 3 pp. Internet website: Accessed July 24, 2007.

U.S. Dept. of the Interior. Fish and Wildlife Service. 2007d. National survey of fishing, hunting, and wildlife-associated recreation. Internet website: http://www.federalaid.fws.gov/surveys/surveys.html. Accessed on July 31, 2007.

U.S. Dept. of the Interior. Geological Survey. 1988. Report to Congress: Coastal barrier resource system. Recommendations for additions to or deletions from the Coastal Barrier Resource System. Vol. 18, Louisiana.

U.S. Dept. of the Interior. Geological Survey. 2006. Extreme storm impact studies. Internet website: http://www.coastal.er.usgs.gov/hurricanes. Accessed June 25, 2007.

U.S. Dept. of the Interior. Geological Survey. 2007a. Hurricane Katrina impact studies. Internet website: http://www.coastal.er.usgs.gov/hurricanes/katrina. Accessed June 22, 2007.

U.S. Dept. of the Interior. Geological Survey. 2007b. Long-term wetland change Florida. Internet website: http://www.coastal.er.usgs.gov/wetlands/. Accessed June 20, 2007.

U.S. Dept. of the Interior. Geological Survey. 2007c. USGS reports latest land change estimates for Louisiana coast. Internet website: http://www.peoplelandandwater.gov/usgs/usgs_02-20-07_usgs-reports-latest.cfm. Accessed July 10, 2007.

U.S. Dept. of the Interior. Geological Survey. 2007d. Gulf of Mexico and southeast tidal wetlands. Internet website: http://www.coastal.er.usgs.gov/wetlands/. Accessed June 27, 2007.

U.S. Dept. of the Interior. Geological Survey. 2007e. USGS Publications Warehouse. Internet website: http://www.pubs.er.usgs.gov/usgspubs. Accessed June 27, 2007.

U.S. Dept. of the Interior. Minerals Management Service. 2001. Outer continental shelf oil & gas leasing program: 2002-2007—final environmental impact statement. 2 vols. U.S. Dept. of the Interior, Minerals Management Service, Herndon, VA. OCS EIS/EA MMS 2002-006.

U.S. Dept. of the Interior. Minerals Management Service. 2005. Environmental Assessment for Independence Hub Surface Facilities and Subsea Development Project Eastern and Central Planning Areas, Gulf of Mexico. U.S. Dept. of the Interior, Minerals Management Service, Gulf of Mexico OCS Region, New Orleans, LA. OCS EIS/EA MMS 2005-064. Internet website: http://www.gomr.mms.gov/homepg/regulate/environ/nepa/MMS2005-064.pdf

U.S. Dept. of the Interior. Minerals Management Service. 2006. Investigations of chemosynthetic communities on the lower continental shelf of the Gulf of Mexico. Ongoing study co-funded by U.S. Dept. of the Interior, Minerals Management Service and U.S. Dept. of Commerce, NOAA, Office of Ocean Exploration. Internet website for the study profile: http://www.gomr.mms.gov/homepg/ regulate/environ/ongoing_studies/gm/GM-05-03.html. Internet website for the *Alvin* cruise from May 7-June 2: http://www.oceanexplorer.noaa.gov/explorations/06mexico/welcome.html.

U.S. Dept. of the Interior. Minerals Management Service. 2007a. Gulf of Mexico OCS oil and gas lease sales: 2007-2012; Western Planning Area Sales 204, 207, 210, 215, and 218; Central Planning Area Sales 205, 206, 208, 213, 216, and 222—final environmental impact statement. 2 vols. U.S. Dept. of the Interior, Minerals Management Service, Gulf of Mexico OCS Region, New Orleans, LA. OCS EIS/EA MMS 2007-018.

U.S. Dept. of the Interior. Minerals Management Service. 2007b. Outer continental shelf oil and gas leasing program, 2007-2012. U.S. Dept. of the Interior, Minerals Management Service, Washington, DC.

U.S. Dept. of the Interior. Minerals Management Service. 2007c. Outer continental shelf oil and gas leasing program: 2007-2012—final environmental impact statement. 2 vols. U.S. Dept. of the Interior, Minerals Management Service, Herndon, VA. OCS EIS/EA MMS 2007-003.

U.S. Dept. of the Interior. Minerals Management Service. 2007d. Gulf of Mexico OCS oil and gas scenario examination: Exploration and development activity. U.S. Dept. of the Interior, Minerals Management Service, Gulf of Mexico OCS Region, New Orleans, LA. OCS Report MMS 2007-052. 14 pp. Internet website: http://www.gomr.mms.gov/PDFs/2007/2007-052.pdf.

U.S. Dept. of the Interior. Minerals Management Service. 2007e. Gulf of Mexico OCS oil and gas scenario examination: Pipeline landfalls. U.S. Dept. of the Interior, Minerals Management Service, Gulf of Mexico OCS Region, New Orleans, LA. OCS Report MMS 2007-053. 5pp. Internet website: http://www.gomr.mms.gov/PDFs/2007/2007-053.pdf

U.S. Dept. of Interior. Minerals Management Service. 2007f. Petroleum spills of one barrel or greater from Federal Outer Continental Shelf facilities resulting from damages caused by 2005 Hurricanes Katrina and Rita including post-hurricane seepage through June 2007. Internet website: http:// www.mms.gov/incidents/PDFs/HurrKatrinaRitaSpillageRev30Jul2007.pdf. Accessed July 30, 2007.

U.S. Dept. of the Interior. Minerals Management Service. 2007g. Estimated petroleum spillage from facilities associated with Federal Outer Continental Shelf (OCS) oil and gas activities resulting from damages caused by Hurricanes Rita and Katrina in 2005. U.S. Dept. of the Interior, Minerals Management Service, Herndon, VA. Internet website: http://www.mms.gov/incidents/PDFs/ HurrKatrinaRitaSpillageRev25Jan2007Final.pdf. Accessed February 1, 2007.

U.S. Dept. of the Interior. Minerals Management Service. 2007h. Minerals Management Service marks hurricane season 2007. News Release, August 30, 2007. U.S. Dept. of the Interior, Minerals Management Service, Gulf of Mexico Region, New Orleans, LA. Internet website: http:// www.gomr.mms.gov/homepg/whatsnew/newsreal/2007/070530.pdf

U.S. Dept. of the Interior. Minerals Management Service. 2007i. Oil-spill risk analysis: Gulf of Mexico Outer Continental Shelf (OCS) lease sales, Central Planning Area and Western Planning Area, 2007-2012 and Gulfwide OCS Program, 2007-2046. U.S. Dept. of the Interior, Minerals Management

Service, Washington, DC. OCS Report MMS 2007-040. Internet website: http://www.mms.gov/itd/pubs/2007/2007-040.pdf

U.S. Dept. of the Interior. Minerals Management Service. 2007j. Biological assessment, USFWS consultation, Gulf of Mexico OCS oil and gas lease sales: 2007-2012. U.S. Dept. of the Interior, Minerals Management Service, Gulf of Mexico OCS Region, New Orleans, LA.

U.S. Dept. of the Interior. Minerals Management Service. 2007k. Five-year meteorological database for the OCD and CALPUFF models. U.S. Dept. of the Interior, Minerals Management Service, Gulf of Mexico Region, New Orleans, LA. OCS Report MMS 2007-067. Internet website: http://www.gomr.mms.gov/homepg/whatsnew/techann/2007/tech2007-067.pdf

U.S. Dept. of the Interior. National Park Service. 2005. November 2005 archeology e-gram. Internet website: http://www.nps.gov/archeology/pubs/egrams/0511.pdf. Accessed July 30, 2007.

U.S. Environmental Protection Agency. 2005. Ozone nonattainment state/area/county report, September 29, 2005. Internet website: http://www.epa.gov/oar/oaqps/greenbk/gncs.html.

U.S. Environmental Protection Agency. 2007a. Phase 2 of the final rule to implement the 8-hour ozone national ambient air quality standard. Final notice of reconsideration. *Federal Register* 72 FR 110, Pp. 31727-31749.

U.S. Environmental Protection Agency. 2007b. 8-hour ozone nonattainment state/area/county report. As of June 20, 2007. Internet website: http://www.epa.gov/oar/oaqps/greenbk/gncs.html.

U.S. Environmental Protection Agency. 2007c. Particulate matter (PM-2.5) nonattainment state/area/county report. As of June 20, 2007. Internet website: http://www.epa.gov/oar/oaqps/greenbk/qncs.html#ALABAMA. Posted October 10, 2007.

U.S. Environmental Protection Agency. 2007d. Offshore and oil & gas NPDES permits, Region 6. Internet website: http://www.epa.gov/Arkansas/6en/w/offshore/home.htm. Accessed July 2, 2007.

U.S. Environmental Protection Agency. 2007e. Oil & gas NPDES permits in the Southeast Region 4. Internet website: http://www.epa.gov/Region4/water/permits/oil&gas.html. Accessed December 17, 2007.

U.S. Environmental Protection Agency. 2007f. National estuary program coastal condition report -- NEP CCR. Internet website: http://www.epa.gov/owow/oceans/nepccr/index.html. Accessed December 17, 2007.

U.S. Environmental Protection Agency. 2007g. USEPA Region 6 NPDES OCS General Permit No. GMG290000. Internet website: http://www.epa.gov/earth1r6/6wq/npdes/genpermt/index.htm. Accessed December 17, 2007.

U.S. Environmental Protection Agency. 2007h. Gulf Hypoxia Action Plan 2008 (DRAFT) for reducing, mitigating, and controlling hypoxia in the northern Gulf of Mexico and improving water quality in the Mississippi River Basin. Mississippi River/Gulf of Mexico Watershed Nutrient Task Force. Internet website: http://www.epa.gov/msbasin/taskforce/pdf/2008draft_actionplan.pdf. Posted November 9, 2007. Accessed December 7, 2007.

Veil, J., T.A. Kimmell, and A.C. Rechner. 2005. Characteristics of produced water discharged to the Gulf of Mexico hypoxic zone. U.S. Dept. of Energy, National Energy Technology Laboratory.

Velando, A., I. Munilla, and P.M. Leyenda. 2005. Short-term indirect effects of the 'Prestige' oil spill on European shags: Changes in availability of prey. Marine Ecology Progress Series 302:263-274.

Walther, D. 2007. Personal communication. Information concerning the status of Gulf sturgeon in the Pearl River, Louisiana, watershed. U.S. Dept. of the Interior, Fish and Wildlife Service, Ecological Services Field Office, Lafayette, LA. May 29, 2007.

White, W.A., T.A. Tremblay, R.L. Waldinger, T.L. Hepner, and T.R. Calnan. 2005. Status and trends of wetland and aquatic habitats on barrier islands, Freeport to East Matagorda Bay and South Padre

Island. Texas General Land Office, Coastal Coordination Division. Internet website: http://www.glo.state.tx.us/coastal/statustrends/freeport-spi/index.html. Accessed June 19, 2007.

White, W.A., T.A. Tremblay, R.L. Waldinger, and T.R. Calnan. 2007. Status of wetlands and aquatic habitats on Texas barriers: Upper Coast Strand Plain Chenier System and Southern Coast Padre Island National Seashore. April 2007. Texas General Land Office, Coastal Coordination Division. Internet website: http://www.glo.state.tx.us/coastal/statustrends/chenier-pims/index.html. Accessed July 9 2007.

Wilson, S. 2007. Personal communication. Information concerning the reissued NPDES general permit. USEPA, Region 6. July 13, 2007.

Wilson, D.L., J.N. Fanjoy, and R.S. Billings. 2004. Gulfwide emission inventory study for the regional haze and ozone modeling efforts: Final report. U.S. Dept. of the Interior, Minerals Management Service, Gulf of Mexico OCS Region, New Orleans, LA. OCS Study 2004-072. 273 pp.

Woods & Poole Economics, Inc. 2006. The 2006 complete economic and demographic data source (CEDDS) on CD-ROM.

Woods & Poole Economics, Inc. 2007. The 2007 complete economic and demographic data source (CEDDS) on CD-ROM.

Zimmer, B., W. Precht, E. Hickerson, and J. Sinclair. 2006. Discovery of *Acropora palmata* at the Flower Garden Banks National Marine Sanctuary, northwestern Gulf of Mexico. Coral Reefs 25(2):192

7. PREPARERS

Supervisors

Dennis L. Chew, Chief, Environmental Assessment Section
Gary D. Goeke, Supervisor, NEPA/CZM Unit
Jack Irion, Supervisor, Social Sciences Unit
Daniel (Herb) Leedy, Supervisor, Biological Sciences Unit
Margaret Metcalf, Supervisor, Physical Sciences Unit
Tara Montgomery, Supervisor, Mapping and Automation Unit
Robert Sebastian, Deputy Regional Supervisor, Leasing and Environment

NEPA Coordination

Thomas W. Bjerstedt, GOMR NEPA Coordinator, Physical Scientist
Mary C. Boatman, Headquarters' NEPA Coordinator, Environmental Specialist

Analysts and Professional Staff

Dave Ball, Marine Archaeologist
Gregory S. Boland, Fisheries Biologist/Biological Oceanographer
Carole L. Current, Physical Oceanographer
Donald (Tre) W. Glenn, III, Protected Species Biologist
Mike Gravois, Geographer
Larry M. Hartzog, Environmental Scientist
Nancy M. Kornrumpf, Program Analyst
Jill Leale, Geographer
Harry Luton, Social Scientist
Stacie Merritt, Meteorologist
Deborah H. Miller, Technical Publications Editor
David P. Moran, Environmental Scientist
Michelle V. Morin, Senior Environmental Scientist
Carol Roden, Protected Species Biologist
Catherine A. Rosa, Environmental Assessment Program Specialist
James Sinclair, Marine Biologist
Kristen L. Strellec, Economist

The Department of the Interior Mission

As the Nation's principal conservation agency, the Department of the Interior has responsibility for most of our nationally owned public lands and natural resources. This includes fostering sound use of our land and water resources; protecting our fish, wildlife, and biological diversity; preserving the environmental and cultural values of our national parks and historical places; and providing for the enjoyment of life through outdoor recreation. The Department assesses our energy and mineral resources and works to ensure that their development is in the best interests of all our people by encouraging stewardship and citizen participation in their care. The Department also has a major responsibility for American Indian reservation communities and for people who live in island territories under U.S. administration.

The Minerals Management Service Mission

As a bureau of the Department of the Interior, the Minerals Management Service's (MMS) primary responsibilities are to manage the mineral resources located on the Nation's Outer Continental Shelf (OCS), collect revenue from the Federal OCS and onshore Federal and Indian lands, and distribute those revenues.

Moreover, in working to meet its responsibilities, the **Offshore Minerals Management Program** administers the OCS competitive leasing program and oversees the safe and environmentally sound exploration and production of our Nation's offshore natural gas, oil and other mineral resources. The MMS **Minerals Revenue Management** meets its responsibilities by ensuring the efficient, timely and accurate collection and disbursement of revenue from mineral leasing and production due to Indian tribes and allottees, States and the U.S. Treasury.

The MMS strives to fulfill its responsibilities through the general guiding principles of: (1) being responsive to the public's concerns and interests by maintaining a dialogue with all potentially affected parties and (2) carrying out its programs with an emphasis on working to enhance the quality of life for all Americans by lending MMS assistance and expertise to economic development and environmental protection.

www.ingramcontent.com/pod-product-compliance
Lightning Source LLC
Chambersburg PA
CBHW080323290526
45790CB00005B/2157